AFRICAN AMERICAN TRAILBLAZERS

Clarence Thomas

Conservative Supreme Court Justice

Ann Byers

Cavendish Square

New York

Published in 2020 by Cavendish Square Publishing, LLC
243 5th Avenue, Suite 136, New York, NY 10016

Library of Congress Cataloging-in-Publication Data

Names: Byers, Ann, author.
Title: Clarence Thomas : conservative Supreme Court justice / Ann Byers.
Description: New York : Cavendish Square, 2019. | Series: African American
trailblazers | Includes bibliographical references and index.
Identifiers: LCCN 2018047207 (print) | LCCN 2018047965 (ebook) | ISBN 9781502645562 (ebook) |
ISBN 9781502645555 (library bound) | ISBN 9781502645548 (pbk.)
Subjects: LCSH: Thomas, Clarence, 1948---Juvenile literature. | United States. Supreme Court--
Officials and employees--Biography--Juvenile literature. | African American judges--Biography--Juvenile
literature. | Judges--United States--Biography--Juvenile literature. |
Political questions and judicial power--United States--Juvenile literature.
Classification: LCC KF8745.T48 (ebook) | LCC KF8745.T48 B94 2019 (print) |
DDC 347.73/2634 [B] --dc23
LC record available at https://lccn.loc.gov/2018047207

Editorial Director: David McNamara
Editor: Kristen Susienka
Copy Editor: Rebecca Rohan
Associate Art Director: Alan Sliwinski
Designer: Joseph Parenteau
Production Coordinator: Karol Szymczuk
Photo Research: J8 Media

CONTENTS

INTRODUCTION

Different Times

O n October 15, 1991, the long, grueling hearings were finally over. The grilling, the cameras, the constant barrage of conflicting testimony—it all had come to an end. More than three months had passed since Clarence Thomas had been nominated to serve on the highest court in the United States, and they had been a blur of excitement, confusion, and profound discouragement. However, the ordeal was over. The Senate had voted to confirm him. Clarence Thomas was the newest associate justice of the United States Supreme Court.

Associate Justice Byron White (*far right*) gives the constitutional oath to Clarence Thomas (*left*) at the White House in October 1991. George Bush (*center rear*), Barbara Bush (*left of Thomas*), and wife Virginia (*right of Thomas*) look on.

Two Oaths

Within a few days of his confirmation, Thomas was sworn in …
twice. All federal judges—judges for cases involving the United
States government and its laws as well as disputes between
states—take two oaths. The first is the Constitutional oath, the
promise to uphold, protect, and defend the US Constitution.
Thomas took this oath three days after his confirmation,
standing next to President and Mrs. George H. W. Bush,
with television cameras rolling. The second oath is the judicial
oath. The judge vows "to administer justice without respect
to persons" and to be fair and impartial "to the poor and to
the rich." Thomas recited this oath in a private ceremony five
days later.[1]

In the week before the justices were to meet and his official
duties would begin, Thomas paid a visit to the man he was
replacing on the Supreme Court, Thurgood Marshall. It was
simply a courtesy, a handoff of responsibilities from one man
to his successor, a passing of the baton from one generation to
the next.

Leaning on a Legacy

Thurgood Marshall and Thomas were alike in a number
of respects. Marshall was the first African American to be
appointed to the Supreme Court. Thomas, his successor, was
only the second. Both were descendants of slaves, and both
bore the scars of racial discrimination. They had both grown
up in segregated neighborhoods, been educated in segregated
schools, and been treated with derision because of their race.
Both had risen above the prejudice to places of honor on the
nation's highest court.

However, the two men were dissimilar in even more ways. Marshall was an icon of the civil rights movement, personally responsible for many of its gains. In his four-year tenure as a judge on the US Court of Appeals, he handed down 112 rulings. He was appointed to the highest court by a Democratic president and confirmed by an impressive 60 to 11 vote of the Senate. Throughout his nearly sixty-year career as a lawyer and a judge, Marshall had gained a reputation as a very liberal champion of racial equality.

After the judicial oath, Thomas takes the traditional walk down the steps of the Supreme Court with Chief Justice William Rehnquist (*left*). He went directly to his first conference as associate justice.

By contrast, Thomas had been a judge for barely a year when nominated to the Supreme Court. He was appointed by a Republican president, edging through a contentious confirmation 52 to 48. As a steadfast conservative, he drew the criticism of many who feared his rulings might reverse some of the achievements of the civil rights movement.

Thomas's courtesy visit to the outgoing justice grew into two and a half hours of lively conversation. When the subject of their differences came up, Marshall put them into perspective: "I did in my time what I had to do. You have to do in your time what you have to do."[2] In the years that followed, as Thomas wrestled with difficult cases, he would often take comfort in Marshall's words.

CHAPTER ONE

The Legacy of Slavery

Thomas's "time" was a century removed from the experience of slavery in the United States. Still, that experience cast a heavy shadow over his life and the lives of countless other African Americans. The system that was part of American life for nearly two hundred fifty years left deep scars on attitudes, actions, institutions, relationships, and laws. When Clarence Thomas was born in 1948, black people were barred from many public places. Blacks and whites lived in different neighborhoods, learned in separate schools, and sat apart from each other on trains and buses. The prejudices deeply rooted in slavery were evident everywhere, especially in the South.

African American workers are photographed on the way to their jobs on a Mississippi cotton farm in 1937. The 6:00 a.m. to 7:00 p.m. job paid a dollar a day.

Legacy of Inequality

When slavery ended, the agricultural economy of the South was no longer sustainable. Landowners had lost their laborers, and the former slaves, called freedmen, had lost their source of food and shelter. To meet the needs of both groups, the sharecropping system emerged.

These men with chains around their legs were African American prisoners in Georgia, leased by the state to a private company to work as a chain gang in the 1880s.

Sharecropping was a simple idea: everyone would share in both the work and the rewards. Former slaves would farm the land in return for a share of the crops. However, the share was never equal. The landowner negotiated with the freedmen for how many acres they would plant and what portion of the crops would be theirs. Because there were plenty of ex-slaves looking for work, the landowner always got the better end of

the bargain. The landowner could not give the sharecropper his share until the harvest, so the sharecropper had to borrow money until the crops came in. By that time, the interest on the loan together with the amount owed often ate up any profit for the sharecropper. For the freedmen, sharecropping was not much different from slavery.

Slavery had not only dominated the economy of the South, but it had also shaped Southern society. In that society, blacks were at the bottom. From the time they were colonies, Southern states had enacted slave codes to keep them there. The codes prohibited slaves from owning property, testifying in court, and gathering together. Some of the codes forbade anyone from teaching a slave to read or write.

When emancipation, the freeing of the slaves, took effect, the slave codes were replaced with the Black Codes. These were basically the same rules by a different name. They contained added provisions about employment, now that African Americans no longer worked for free. In some Southern states, freedmen could work only on farms owned by white people or as their servants. In some places, they could hold other jobs, but to do so they had to pay a high price for a license. In all the Southern states, any black man found not working could be arrested and jailed. To get a job, the freedmen often had to sign unfair contracts, and if they broke the contract by leaving their employment, they could be hunted down and forced to return. Life under the Black Codes was much the same as under slavery.

States were within their legal rights to enact these codes. The only thing the law—specifically the Thirteenth Amendment—said was that slavery should no longer exist in the United States. Technically, the freedmen of the South were not slaves. However, federal law could overrule state law.

In order to secure for African Americans the benefits of their freedom, Congress passed the Fourteenth Amendment. It became law in 1868.

The Fourteenth Amendment reaffirmed that former slaves were now US citizens: "All persons born or naturalized in the United States, and subject to the jurisdiction thereof, are citizens of the United States and of the state wherein they reside." It nullified any state legislation that denied the former slaves their rights: "No state shall make or enforce any law which shall abridge the privileges or immunities of citizens of the United States." It guaranteed that former slaves could not have their property taken from them or be put in jail without a fair trial; it promised them the same protections as every other citizen: "nor shall any state deprive any person of life, liberty, or property, without due process of law; nor deny to any person within its jurisdiction the equal protection of the laws."

Shortly after the Fourteenth Amendment became law, Congress passed the Fifteenth Amendment, providing that "the right of citizens of the United States to vote shall not be denied or abridged by the United States or by any State on account of race, color, or previous condition of servitude."

Despite the federal laws, some white people refused to accept the equality of blacks and whites. A small group formed a club to resist the enforcement of the laws. Named for the Greek word for "circle," *kyklos*, they called themselves the Ku Klux Klan, or KKK. Their goals were to keep African Americans from voting and to maintain white rule. They dressed in long, white robes with pointed hoods that covered their faces. They began by frightening freedmen and their families and threatening any white people who tried to help the former slaves. The intimidation quickly led to violence. Members of the KKK burned black churches, destroyed black schools, and broke into homes. The group spread to every Southern state. By the 1920s, the Klan numbered more than four million.

Legacy of Separation

The entrenched attitude of racial inequality led inevitably to segregation, or racial separation. White people who believed they were better than blacks did not want to associate with them. To ensure that whites would have as little contact with blacks as possible, Southern states passed a series of laws that mandated segregation. The laws required not only separate schools, but also separate libraries, restrooms, and water fountains. Public buildings had separate doors for blacks and whites; trains had separate ticket windows and separate waiting rooms. These regulations became known as Jim Crow laws. They were named for a character in a traveling theater performance that made fun of African Americans. Begun in the 1870s, many of the Jim Crow laws were enforced until 1965. They made segregation in the Southern states not only legal but required.

Instead of overruling the Jim Crow laws with federal legislation, those fighting segregation decided to challenge the laws in court. To challenge a law, someone has to break that law and be tried; he can claim he is innocent of wrongdoing because the law is unconstitutional. To test the Jim Crow laws, an mixed-race man named Homer Plessy boarded a train and sat in a "whites only" car. That action violated the Louisiana Separate Car Act, and Plessy was arrested.

The judge ruled that the law was constitutional. Plessy appealed to the state's highest court and then to the Supreme Court. The trial was called *Plessy v. Ferguson* because Judge John Ferguson was the lower court judge. Plessy's lawyers argued

Some Jim Crow practices were enforced in and beyond the Southern states. This "for colored only" drinking fountain was in a streetcar terminal in Oklahoma in 1939.

that the Fourteenth Amendment guarantees equal treatment to all citizens, and the Separate Car Act denied him the same rights it gave white citizens. The justices agreed with the lower court. They said providing a separate train car was fair because it was equal to the cars reserved for white passengers. This 1896 case spelled out the doctrine of "separate but equal" that would make segregation legal in the entire country for the next fifty-eight years.

Battling the Legacy

Plessy v. Ferguson sanctioned the segregation that was everywhere in the South, but other parts of the country did not have Jim Crow laws. Nor did they have sharecropping or Klan violence. African Americans looked to move to the cities of the North, Midwest, and West for relief from oppression and for economic and social opportunity. World War I opened those opportunities for them.

When the war began in 1914, American companies were supplying war materials for the conflict in Europe. However, the war put an end to the steady stream of immigrants, many of whom worked in those companies. When the United States entered the war in 1917, men left the factories for the battlefields, and the labor shortage became even more severe. Manufacturers, desperate for workers, recruited African Americans from the South. When the war ended, black families continued to move north and west in what became known as the Great Migration. By 1930, two million blacks had left the South, and by 1970, the number had risen to six million.

In the North and the West, African Americans made more money than they had in the South, but they did not escape discrimination, inequality, and separation. Some hotels would not rent rooms to blacks, and some restaurants and theaters designated specific sections for them. Banks often refused to lend to African Americans or charged them exorbitant interest. People in white neighborhoods formed agreements to sell their homes only to whites. The segregation was not enforced by law, as it was in the South, but it was nonetheless real.

In addition to jobs, World War I gave African Americans the chance to serve in the army. Some considered military service their duty as citizens; others hoped it would prove their worth and lead to respect and equal treatment. Many thought it might produce a more just society. After all, the war was billed as a crusade to make the world "safe for democracy," a fight for "the liberation of its people," a struggle to "make the world itself at last free."[1] In the expectation that they would be part of bringing that vision of true freedom and equality to their own country, 370,000 African Americans served in the US Army during the war.

However, they found neither acceptance nor fairness in the military. The army, like every American institution, was segregated. The all-black regiments were not sent into battle; they were assigned to support positions such as cooking and cleaning or to labor battalions, building roads and storage facilities, and loading and unloading supplies. African Americans complained so loudly about the unequal treatment that the army reluctantly formed two all-black combat units. When given the chance to actually take up arms, the men performed admirably. Although the United States did not recognize the bravery and competence of its African American soldiers, France awarded them several medals in appreciation of their heroism.

After the war, white soldiers came home to cheering crowds; black soldiers returned to the same prejudices they had left. Their victory in battle had not brought true democracy to the United States. W. E. B. Du Bois, a strong voice in the black community, summed up the frustration of African Americans in 1919. In an article in the *Crisis*, the magazine of the National Association for the Advancement of Colored People (NAACP), he catalogued what he and other blacks felt was bad about their country. He called America a shameful land that "lynches … disenfranchises its own citizens … encourages ignorance … steals from us … insults us … and it

ORGANIZING FOR RACIAL EQUALITY

The oldest and largest organization in the United States working for racial justice was actually begun by white people. They were reformers and journalists angered by stories of widespread violence against African Americans. The final straw for the little group came in 1908—a murderous rampage against a black community in Springfield, Illinois, a Northern city. The group called for others to join them in figuring out how to end the injustice. The result was the National Association for the Advancement of Colored People—the NAACP. Its purpose was to ensure that the promises of the Thirteenth, Fourteenth, and Fifteenth Amendments were extended to all Americans. The organization was formed in 1909, on February 12, Abraham Lincoln's birthday.

One of the founders of the NAACP, and its only African American officer, was sociologist and professor W. E. B. Du Bois. Du Bois began a magazine called the *Crisis*. Its purpose was to present information detailing incidents of racial prejudice and give suggestions for ways to bring true democracy to Americans of every color. In time, the publication added poetry and other writings of black artists, celebrating the richness of African American culture. For people suffering bigotry, the *Crisis* became a source of pride, a rallying cry, and a beacon of hope.

The NAACP also took action. It launched a campaign to expose and end the lynching of black people. When lawyer Thurgood Marshall joined the organization in 1934, he created a legal defense fund and, together with other lawyers, won for African Americans other rights they had been denied. The NAACP grew from nine thousand members in 1917 to ninety thousand in 1919, and it continues strong to this day.

looks upon any attempt to question or even discuss this dogma as arrogance … and treason."[2]

Du Bois was not afraid to question the dogma of inequality, and he called on all African Americans to do the same. He urged them to question it with action, to oppose it with physical force if necessary. He warned the country that the troops who had fought for the freedom of people in Europe were determined to experience freedom in their own land. He wrote, "We *return from fighting. We return fighting.*"[3]

Crossing the Color Line

The fighting started almost the minute the troops arrived back in the United States. The first battles were over the "color line," an invisible wall that separated blacks from whites. On one side were decent neighborhoods, steady jobs with good pay, and opportunities for advancement. On the other side were high-priced, substandard housing and dead-end, menial labor positions. Black people were expected to stay in their "place," on their side of the line. But fighting overseas had given them the courage to ignore the imaginary barrier. The African American soldiers who had fought in France had been regarded as liberators and treated with respect and gratitude. This gave them a sense of dignity they were denied in America.

When the returning soldiers and other blacks expressed their newfound pride—in one instance by simply wearing their army uniforms—whites branded them as "uppity" and attempted to put them back in their "place." Insolent words, small scuffles, and rumored offenses sparked heated confrontations and mushroomed into major disturbances. In one year alone, violent incidents of whites attacking blacks shook more than thirty cities across the country. The race riots were so bloody in the summer

The 369th Infantry Regiment, seen here returning to New York after World War I, was nicknamed the Harlem Hellfighters. The group spent more time on the front lines than any other American unit.

of 1919, with more than 165 deaths, that black leader James Weldon Johnson labeled those months the "Red Summer."

Undeterred, blacks continued to step over the color line, pressing for the rights that belonged to them as citizens. Progress was painfully slow. The first major success came among African Americans working as railroad porters for the Pullman Company. Porters were attendants who served people on trains. Trains had sleeping cars with beds that allowed passengers to travel long distances in comfort. Porters made up the beds, loaded and unloaded passengers' luggage, served food and drinks, and kept the cars clean. Their pay was low and their working conditions poor. Convinced the only way the porters could improve their circumstances was to join together, A. Philip Randolph organized them into a labor union in 1925, the Brotherhood of Sleeping Car Porters.

The Pullman Company resisted Randolph's efforts, but after a ten-year struggle, it finally agreed to negotiate with the union. The Brotherhood won higher wages, overtime pay, and a shorter workweek for the black porters. This was less than what Pullman's white conductors and other employees had, but it was a giant step closer to equal treatment.

Randolph pushed for more. If a union of hundreds of blacks could force concessions from a huge company, a band of thousands should be able to gain similar benefits from the government. Randolph targeted the defense industry, companies making weapons for the military. These private companies that had contracts with the federal government refused to hire African Americans. Randolph threatened to march to Washington, DC with 100,000 black men unless President Franklin Roosevelt did something to force the companies to remove the ban against African Americans. The year was 1941, the country was preparing for the likelihood of war, and Roosevelt could not afford any disruption in the defense industry. He issued Executive Order 8802, declaring there would be no discrimination in hiring in the defense industry or in any government agency. This marked another major win for Randolph and for racial equality.

When America entered World War II at the end of that year, blacks faced the same prejudices and separations they had encountered in World War I. Randolph and others continued to lobby for fairness. Their persistence was eventually rewarded. In 1948, President Harry Truman signed Executive Order 9981, which put an end to segregation in the armed forces. The color line was beginning to fade.

Toward Liberty and Justice for All

The artificial line was erased, at least legally, in 1954 with the *Brown v. Board of Education of Topeka* Supreme Court decision. That ruling overturned the "separate but equal" doctrine, making segregation in schools illegal in every state. However, it took federal troops, court orders, and ten years to fully enforce the decision. It required a decades-long civil rights movement to secure laws that eventually prohibited racial separation in housing, transportation, and other areas. Achieving civil rights came at the price of arrests, beatings, bombings, and deaths. But it came.

Clarence Thomas was born in 1948, one year after baseball great Jackie Robinson broke the color line in sports. The civil rights movement was still a decade away. The world into which Thomas was born was an America slowly and reluctantly emerging from the worst of slavery's legacy. It was a country that was still far short of its promise of justice and equal rights for all its citizens. But it was moving closer.

CHAPTER TWO

His Grandfather's Son

In Clarence Thomas's judicial chambers sits a bronze bust of a little-known black man. He was not a judge, a politician, or a great leader, yet his image occupies a place of honor in Thomas's office. The grandson of slaves, this man had no title, no fortune, no famous achievement. Thomas has rubbed shoulders with heads of large universities and major corporations, directors of high-level government agencies, and at least six American presidents, but he describes the figure in bronze as the only hero in his life, "the greatest man I have ever known."[1] To his friends and neighbors, the man was Myers Anderson; Thomas called him "Daddy."

At the beginning of his confirmation hearings before the Senate Judiciary Committee, on October 10, 1991, an admittedly nervous Clarence Thomas raises his right hand and swears to testify truthfully.

The First Role Model

Anderson became "Daddy" when Thomas was just seven years old. Thomas's biological father had left long ago, and his mother had moved her family from rural Pin Point, Georgia, where Thomas had been born, to a run-down tenement in Savannah. The apartment was not quite three blocks from the house of her father, Myers Anderson, who was also Thomas's grandfather. The meager wages Thomas's mother received as a maid did not always stretch far enough to feed her three children. So she sent the younger two—Thomas and his little brother, Myers—to live with their grandfather and his wife.

To a seven-year-old who had never known a father, Myers Anderson seemed stern. His rules were strict, and he tolerated no backtalk. Except for the time spent in school, the boys were almost never out of his sight. Anderson took them with him as he made his rounds delivering fuel oil. He told them that learning to work hard would be their inheritance.

Anderson went to great lengths to see that his boys knew how to work and stayed out of trouble. His family owned a plot of neglected land about half an hour from Savannah. In Thomas's ninth summer, when his brother Myers was eight, Anderson and his two "sons" turned the fields into a farm. They built a four-room house, a barn, and other buildings. They cut down trees, cleared the land, and broke up the soil with a horse-drawn plow. They planted sugarcane, corn, beans, and other vegetables. These, together with the chickens and hogs they raised and the game Anderson hunted, would sustain them through the summer and be preserved for the winter ahead. Until Thomas left home ten years later, he spent every summer on the farm, from the moment school ended in June until the day before it resumed in September.

The Sweetfield of Eden Baptist Church, founded in 1897 and rebuilt in 1961, is one of the landmarks of Pin Point, Georgia. Near the church is a museum celebrating the community settled by former slaves from nearby islands.

Years later, Thomas described the values that defined his upbringing: "God was central. School, discipline, hard work, and knowing right from wrong were of the highest priority. Crime, welfare, slothfulness, and alcohol were enemies."[2] Throughout his childhood, if he dared complain that any assignment was too difficult, his grandfather would recite the words now engraved beneath the chiseled features on the bronze plaque: "Old Man Can't is dead—I helped bury him."

Introduction to a White World

Almost as important as hard work in the Anderson home was education. Thomas's grandfather, who had not gone beyond the third grade, was determined his boys would have the best schooling he could afford. He knew it was the only way they could get a "coat-and-tie job," a chance for a better life than he had. He decided Catholic schools offered not only the best education, but also the strictest discipline. Besides, unlike most other African Americans in Georgia, who were Baptist, Anderson was Catholic.

At the time, all schools in Savannah, both public and Catholic, were segregated. Segregation had been declared illegal in 1954, the year Thomas started school, but Georgia was among the states slow to implement the mandate of *Brown v. Board of Education*. So from first through tenth grade, Thomas attended all-black Catholic schools. The white nuns taught that all men, black and white, were created equal. They pushed him to do his very best and made him believe he could do anything as well as any white person. However, in his segregated world, he had little chance to test that belief. That is, until in tenth grade he decided he wanted to become a priest.

Thomas decided to stay in the South, opting to apply to St. John Vianney, the only high school in the area that prepared young men for careers as priests. He was one of two black seminarians there. After St. John's, he went to a college seminary in Missouri, where he would complete his training.

Living in the seminary thrust Thomas for the first time into a white world. He found himself face-to-face with stares, whispers, and stifled laughs. He often felt alone in the midst of groups of students, the victim of pranks, and sometimes the subject of jokes he didn't understand. His response was to bury Old Man Can't and plunge into his studies. He discovered that, at least academically, he could do every bit as well as any of his white classmates. It was not pleasant, but he could survive—in fact, he could thrive—in a white world.

An Angry Young Man

Something else happened to Thomas during his time at the seminary. He became aware of what was going on outside his narrow sphere. The segregation of Savannah and the ignorance of youth had kept him from understanding the struggles of African Americans. He had been oblivious to the pain and injustice beyond his comfortable dorm room, but now he saw it. He was troubled that no one in the Catholic Church seemed to be standing up against it.

The breaking point came for him on the day Martin Luther King Jr. was killed. Several students were together on campus when another student burst in and announced that King had been shot. More hurtful to Thomas than the devastating news was a classmate's reaction: "I hope he dies," he said.

How could anyone wish a good man dead, he questioned. How could a religious person, someone planning to be a priest, rejoice in something evil? Didn't he understand the horrendous treatment of African Americans Dr. King had been working to correct? The student, the seminary, the Church—all seemed completely divorced from reality, at least the reality of human suffering.

The event completely shattered Thomas. That same week, he marched in his very first civil rights demonstration. As he chanted and sang, he felt the energy of the thousands beside him. He felt the pain of black brothers he did not know; he felt the righteousness of their cause. *This*, he decided, as opposed to the artificial realm of self-proclaimed religious people offering compassionless prayers, *this* was real. This was meaningful. Thomas decided he no longer wanted to be a priest.

Thomas left the seminary and returned to Savannah. He found a job with a company that made paper bags. That summer, he experienced the full brunt of what Dr. King had fought so hard against. He bristled under the scowls of his white bosses and the taunts of his white coworkers. He seethed at the ugly racial slurs carved into bathroom walls and the KKK signs posted in prominent places. He resented the clear message that no matter what he did, he was not and never would be as good as a white man. He "closed out the [19]60s," he later said, "as one angry young man."[3]

Rage and Reason

Meanwhile, a Catholic priest 875 miles (1,406 kilometers) away was also angry over racial inequities. Reverend John Brooks, vice president of College of the Holy Cross, was determined to give African Americans the chance to prove they were just as capable as anyone else. Immediately after King's assassination, he began to recruit young black men to the then all-white, all-male school. He arranged for financial aid so promising students like Thomas could accept his offer.

What attracted Thomas to Holy Cross was not its prestige or its high academic standing, but its location in Worcester, Massachusetts. Thomas had heard that blacks in the North were more militant in their pursuit of racial justice than those in the South. Many in the South seemed to accept the inferior place allotted to them rather than fight for the equality that was rightfully theirs. Thomas wanted to fight.

At Holy Cross, the angry young man joined with the few African Americans there to create a Black Students' Union. He participated in protests and demonstrations. He adopted the clothing, language, and indignation of the radical black power movement. The speeches of Louis Farrakhan and the writings of Malcolm X fueled his rage.

Between the protests and his schoolwork, Thomas met a freshman at a nearby school for women. Kathy Ambush was just as committed to racial justice as Thomas, and just as active. They dated for several months and set a wedding date for the day after his graduation.

Toward the end of his junior year, Thomas took part in a protest march that spun out of control. The two-hour riot ended in fires, looting, tear gas, more than three hundred injuries, thirty-five arrests, and $100,000 in damages. The next day, away from the frenzy of the crowd, Thomas was appalled at what he had done. The chanting, the defiance, the destruction were exhilarating, but they had accomplished nothing. No war had stopped, no prisoner had been freed. Not a single black life had been improved. Why had he allowed emotion to sweep him up in meaningless violence?

The incident—and his participation in it—troubled him. He was still enraged over the bigotry that kept African Americans oppressed, but he realized that anger was not achieving anything for them. The anger was feeding the prejudices in society, and it was destroying him in the process. He had to get rid of the anger; he had to find another way to fight what he knew was a worthy cause.

As he wrestled with the powerlessness of brute force, it dawned on him that he had another weapon: his intellect. God had given him a sharp mind, and the nuns and priests had given him a solid education. He could use his skill at logic, his ability

Thomas marched in the April 1970 antiwar demonstration in Harvard Square in Cambridge, Massachusetts, where two thousand police clad in riot gear used tear gas and clubs to calm a crowd of three thousand rioters.

to analyze and reason, to help his black brothers and sisters. He decided to become a lawyer.

Thomas abandoned his civil rights activities and spent his last year at Holy Cross immersed in his studies. He graduated cum laude—with honor—with a degree in English literature. He applied to two of the best law schools in the country, Harvard and Yale, and was accepted at both. He thought Harvard a bit too conservative, so he chose Yale.

The three years of law school were tougher than anything Thomas had faced so far. He was newly married, and Kathy gave birth to a son—his only child—in the middle of his second year

This is the clock tower at College of the Holy Cross. The school began in 1843 with six students. Today, it has nearly three thousand students and is recognized as one of the finest liberal arts colleges in the United States.

at Yale. Financial aid covered the cost of his tuition, but it did not pay for an apartment, food, or diapers. So Thomas worked fifteen hours a week at New Haven Legal Assistance, helping low-income members of the community, predominantly African Americans. At the same time, he was carrying a large course load of difficult subjects.

Despite the pressures, he made it through, earning a Doctor of Jurisprudence (JD) degree in 1974. Twenty years of schooling had at last come to a close. It was time to find a job.

A Coat-and-Tie Job

Finding a job was not as easy as Thomas had thought it would be. He interviewed with law firms in Atlanta, Washington, New York, and Los Angeles. But no one wanted to hire him. His classmates were all receiving offers, and Thomas had better grades than many of them. It took several interviews for him to figure out why he was being rejected. The lawyers interviewing him thought he had not really earned the good grades on his transcript. They suspected the only way he had been able to attend Yale was through the school's affirmative action program.

Affirmative action is a policy of preferential treatment of minorities. Beginning in 1961, the federal government required that companies receiving government money take affirmative action—that is, do something intentional—to ensure that minorities had the same opportunities in the workplace as everyone else. The mandate quickly spread beyond employment into education and beyond government concerns into private companies and universities. The thinking was that because minorities had been kept behind others through discrimination, they should be given an extra boost to enable

MEN – AND WOMEN –
IN BLACK

There are no rules that require Supreme Court justices to wear black robes. Yet this has been their attire almost since the first court sat in 1790. Judges in England, the model for America's judiciary, wore robes, so dressing in robes made sense for US courts. In England, however, the robes were often colorful, sometimes flamboyant. The first US Supreme Court justice, John Jay, wore a black-and-salmon-colored robe. However, according to legend, Thomas Jefferson felt that bright colors were pretentious and judges should dress modestly. And so they did and still do. It is tradition that prescribes the wearing of black robes.

That is not to say the judges cannot display some individuality. Sandra Day O'Connor, the first female justice, added a white collar to her black robe. Chief Justice William Rehnquist, imitating a character in a Gilbert and Sullivan opera, had gold stripes sewn onto one of his sleeves. Ruth Bader Ginsburg often wears a colorful ruffle or collar over her robe.

After the judges don their black robes, before they walk into the courtroom, each of the nine justices shakes hands with every other justice. The judges often disagree with one another in their decisions, but this custom reminds them they are a team with the common goal of delivering justice to all who seek it from them.

them to catch up. The extra boost was usually preference in hiring and promotions. It might mean hiring a person who did not have all the qualifications needed for a particular job … or admitting an African American to a college even if he did not have the test scores required.

The men who interviewed Thomas assumed his high grades in a top-notch school reflected racial preference rather than academic excellence. They could not be sure he was as good as his record suggested. When Thomas realized this bigoted notion was at the root of his difficulty getting a job, the old anger returned. He may have gotten into Yale because of affirmative action, but he earned every one of his grades through hard work. He knew the truth, but he had no way to prove himself to others. In frustration, he peeled a fifteen-cent price tag off a package of cigars and stuck it to the frame of his law school certificate. That, he fumed, was what a law degree from Yale was worth when viewed through the lens of affirmative action.

Despite the huge strike against him, Thomas had no choice but to keep putting in applications. He heard the attorney general of Missouri was coming to Yale looking for new lawyers for his staff. Thomas did not have much hope of impressing him. The man was rich, born into a wealthy family, a success by age thirty-two; how could he relate to a black man from Pin Point, Georgia, desperate for a job? Besides, he was a Republican. Since the beginning of the civil rights movement, African Americans had been almost exclusively Democrats. No black person Thomas knew, and very few of his classmates at Yale, were Republican. If he even had a chance, could he work for a Republican?

He would soon find out. John Danforth offered him a job as an assistant attorney general, arguing criminal and civil cases in the Supreme Court of Missouri on behalf of the state.

A Black Republican

In Missouri, Thomas honed his legal skills. He researched and argued cases and wrote briefs, opinions, and other court documents. He spoke confidently and well in the courtroom. He also received praise for his work from judges and other lawyers, as well as from his boss. After three years, when Danforth left his position as state attorney general to run for the US Senate, Thomas received numerous job offers. At last, his abilities were being recognized.

Thomas tried practicing corporate law for a while, working for Monsanto, the chemical giant headquartered in St. Louis. It was a huge operation with many opportunities for moving around and learning new things. The pay was good, which was important because Thomas was struggling under a massive load of debt, largely from college loans. However, the work was not fulfilling. What he really wanted to do was use his talents to help struggling African Americans.

Thomas's dissatisfaction on the job was mirrored by discontent at home. To deal with his frustrations, Thomas began drinking heavily, a practice that would continue for a few more years. What pulled him out of his depression was a call from John Danforth, now a US senator from Missouri. Danforth asked Thomas to come to Washington, DC, to serve as one of his legislative assistants. Thomas jumped at the offer.

As he thought about what he could do in Washington to better the lives of ordinary African Americans, Thomas questioned the solutions the government was offering. The government's answer for the poor academic performance of so many blacks was integrating the schools by busing some black children to white schools and some white children to black schools. But Thomas had gotten good grades in both segregated and integrated schools. Perhaps racial separation itself was not the problem, but the fact that separation led to unequal educations. Maybe the solution was not integration, but better schools for everybody.

The government's remedies for inequality in the workplace were racial quotas and affirmative action. Thomas's bitter personal experience convinced him these approaches did more harm than good. As Thomas saw it, government programs to help minorities took away their will to work, as well as their self-respect. They stripped people of what they actually needed to succeed: self-reliance and a can-do attitude.

Thomas's thinking was changing from the liberal ideas of his college days to the conservative philosophy of his grandfather. The liberals he knew, especially in the black community, thought African Americans had been treated so poorly for so long that the government had a responsibility to right the wrongs. But, Thomas felt, they were blind to the negative effects of the "fixes." Conservatives believed the government should be involved as little as possible in people's lives. That was how Thomas's grandfather had raised him—to depend on himself and his neighbors.

Thomas could not talk about these views because almost no one shared them, at least hardly anyone he knew, and certainly no other African American. That is, until he discovered the writings of Thomas Sowell. Sowell, an African American economist and social theorist, articulated the very ideas Thomas was thinking. Thomas was thrilled to find a black man who proclaimed boldly what he believed was the truth about the government's well-intentioned but flawed and ineffective attempts to bring about racial equality. In time, he would find others.

However, Sowell and the few people like him were criticized harshly. It appeared to Thomas that every African American was expected to say that government programs were the antidote

Thomas appears in the Oval Office with President Ronald Reagan (*left*) in 1986 after being confirmed by the Senate to serve a second four-year term as EEOC chairman.

to racial injustice and to demand more of them. Any who disagreed were branded traitors to the race. Thomas was afraid to speak out publicly. But he did take what for him was an enormous step away from black group-think. He changed his political affiliation. In order to vote for Ronald Reagan in his 1980 bid for his party's nomination for president, he registered as a Republican.

From Coat to Robe

For the most part, Thomas kept his unorthodox views to himself. In Danforth's office, he worked on issues involving energy and the environment, not racial justice. Few of his colleagues knew his positions regarding civil rights. However, that changed when he attended a conference at which he was seated next to Juan Williams, a young black reporter for the *Washington Post*. He mentioned to Williams his disagreement with federal policies for correcting racial disparities. He never dreamed the reporter would print his casual comments in his newspaper. However, black conservatives were rare in 1980, and Thomas's opinions were newsworthy, so Williams's story thrust the legislative assistant into the national spotlight. When Thomas returned to Washington, he was met with hostility from many.

Not everyone disapproved of Thomas's stance. The story attracted the attention of President Reagan, who asked Thomas to serve in his Department of Education as assistant secretary for civil rights. After he had spent a year in that position, the president moved him to the Equal Employment Opportunity Commission (EEOC). He worked as its chairman for eight years, until called upon by a new president, this time not only for a new job but for a new career. George H. W. Bush, the elder Bush president, appointed Thomas as a judge on the US Court of Appeals for the District of Columbia.

A Supreme Test

Just sixteen months into Thomas's new job, Supreme Court Justice Thurgood Marshall resigned. Some of the eight remaining justices tended to be liberal, and conservative President Bush wanted a conservative judge to replace Marshall. On July 1, 1991, he nominated Clarence Thomas for the position.

That announcement sparked howls of protest from liberal groups. Some complained that Thomas, at forty-three, was too young to be able to make good decisions. Others pointed out that he had been a judge for less than eighteen months and was therefore too inexperienced. Most of the objections

Senator Joe Biden, chairman of the Senate Judiciary Committee, interrogates Thomas on the second day of his Supreme Court confirmation hearing as Senator Ted Kennedy (*right*) awaits his turn.

were over his conservative views, particularly regarding race; he did not trust government involvement in race matters. The NAACP refused to support him. Many painted him as the anti–Thurgood Marshall, warning that he would roll back all the liberties Marshall had won for African Americans.

Nominees for all federal judgeships have to be confirmed by the Senate. Confirmation is a two-step process. First, the Judiciary Committee, composed of fourteen senators in 1991, interviews the nominee and votes on whether to recommend the nominee to the full Senate. Second, the full Senate discusses the nominee and then votes to confirm or reject him or her.

Confirmation hearings for Thomas were contentious. Some of the senators who did not want Thomas on the court asked questions to trip him up or make him look bad. They had sent their staff to Thomas's former colleagues, trying to find dirt they could use to smear him. One asked reporter Juan Williams, "Have you got anything on your tapes we can use to stop Thomas?"[4] Thomas endured five withering days of questioning from the Senate Judiciary.

Then, two days before the Senate was scheduled to vote, a bombshell stopped the proceedings cold. Anita Hill, a law professor who had worked with Thomas at both the Department of Education and the EEOC, accused the judge of sexually harassing her at those agencies. The FBI had investigated her charges and, finding no corroboration, had dismissed them. However, someone leaked Hill's claims to a reporter, and she repeated them on National Public Radio. The Senate Judiciary Committee reopened the hearings for three more days of questioning.

Those sessions, televised to the entire nation, were lurid. Hill said Thomas had talked to her many times about his sexual interests, and she described those interests in unpleasant and graphic detail. She testified that he had never touched her or threatened to fire her, but his conversations had made her uncomfortable. Thomas expressed complete surprise and utter disbelief. He insisted none of the allegations were true.

Thomas had been through many storms in his life. He had struggled with drinking and beaten it. He had left his wife, a decision he forever regretted. But this was worse. This was an attack on his character, on his name. This was an attempt to silence a voice and a perspective with which some disagreed. He felt crushed beneath the weight of these events and accusations. When invited to make a statement, Thomas said

Anita Hill testifies at Thomas's confirmation hearing in 1991. At the time, she was a law professor at the University of Oklahoma.

he would speak not because he wanted the job, but to clear his reputation. He adamantly denied the charges leveled against him. He added:

> This is a circus. It is a national disgrace. And from my standpoint, as a black American, as far as I am concerned, it is a high-tech lynching for uppity-blacks who in any way deign to think for themselves, to do for themselves, to have different ideas.[5]

In the end, it was a classic case of "he said, she said." There were no witnesses to any of the alleged conversations. Hill produced witnesses who said she told them of the harassment, but people questioned whether those events occurred. Others testified for Thomas, saying they never saw anything of the type Hill claimed, but that did not mean it didn't happen. There was no way to know the truth, but the senators had to vote. Years later, John Sununu, President Bush's chief of staff during the hearings, explained how he and some others decided. He said the people who knew Anita Hill believed her, the people who knew Thomas believed him, and the people who knew them both believed Thomas. When the Senate finally voted, Thomas was confirmed by one of the narrowest margins of any Supreme Court justice: 52 to 48.

CHAPTER THREE

Team of Nine

I n his nearly thirty years on the Supreme Court, Clarence Thomas has served with sixteen other justices, twelve men and four women. They have come from different parts of the country and a variety of backgrounds. They do not all share the same judicial philosophy; their thinking about the law ranges from liberal, or left-leaning, to ultra conservative, or far right. They have different interests, different tastes, and different lives outside the courtroom. Despite their many dissimilarities and frequent disagreements, the justices

The Supreme Court chamber is the place where the most serious legal cases are brought to be judged.

work together cordially, in an atmosphere that is warm and friendly. The traditional handshake that precedes every session and every conference is genuine.

Oldest Friendship

The person with whom Thomas served the longest was Anthony Kennedy. Kennedy came to the court just three years before Thomas, and they worked together for twenty-seven years before Kennedy retired in 2018. They couldn't be more different. Thomas was from the rural South; Kennedy grew up around politics in Sacramento and San Francisco, California. His father was a lawyer and a lobbyist, and his mother was involved in civic affairs. Before enrolling in Stanford University, Kennedy was a page in the California Senate, delivering messages and papers to the legislators.

Kennedy's legal background before being nominated to the Supreme Court was far more extensive than Thomas's. He was not only a practicing attorney, but he also ran a law practice and taught constitutional law. He served on a number of federal judicial committees and as an appellate judge for twelve years. Unlike Thomas, Kennedy enjoyed a relatively smooth transition to the Supreme Court, confirmed 97 to 0.

The differences in background did not keep the two justices from enjoying a long friendship. Kennedy sometimes expressed liberal opinions and at other times conservative views. He was often called the swing vote because the general public could seldom predict which way he would go. One point of departure between the two was Kennedy's tendency to sometimes look to the practices of other countries to guide his thinking about whether a law was just or wise. In Kennedy's final year on the Supreme Court, Thomas voted with him 83 percent of the time.

The Chiefs

When Thomas first came to the court, the chief justice was William Rehnquist. At that point, he had been an associate justice for fourteen years and the chief justice for five. He was already somewhat of a legend. At the beginning of his tenure, as a conservative on a mostly liberal court, he dissented from the majority opinion so many times he earned the nickname "The

As chief justice, John Roberts is responsible for the administration of the entire federal court system. If he is in the majority on an opinion, he chooses which justice writes the opinion.

Lone Ranger." When new appointments made the court more conservative, Rehnquist gained a reputation as a fair, even-handed leader. He was praised for his organizational efficiency and respected for his near-obsessive insistence on punctuality. Rehnquist and Thomas served together fourteen years.

Thomas has served about as long with Rehnquist's replacement as chief justice, John Roberts. By the time he was appointed to the Supreme Court, Roberts knew a good deal about that body. He had been a law clerk for Associate Justice Rehnquist. Law clerks are responsible for legal research, some writing, proofreading, and other assignments for judges. They are usually recent graduates of law schools getting their first experience in the legal profession. After clerking for Rehnquist, Roberts had jobs in which he presented cases before the court, both as a private attorney and as a government lawyer. He served as a judge on the US Court of Appeals for two years before being nominated for the higher court.

Although Roberts and Thomas are both conservative, Thomas is more so. Roberts has made a number of decisions with which Thomas disagreed. In 2017, the two were in agreement 79 percent of the time.

Four Women

Although Thomas has had considerably less agreement with his female colleagues, he has some experiences in common with Sandra Day O'Connor, the first woman to serve on the Supreme Court. Both had rural beginnings, Thomas in Georgia, O'Connor in Texas. Both were raised, at least partly, by their grandparents. O'Connor's parents thought their daughter would receive a better education in a city, so they sent her to El Paso to live with her grandparents. Like Thomas,

PRESERVING INDEPENDENCE

The federal judicial system consists of three levels. At the lowest level are ninety-four district courts; these are trial courts at which judges hear cases for the first time. If one of the parties that brought a case to the district court is unhappy with the judges' decision, that party may appeal to the next level, the circuit court. There are thirteen circuit courts, also called appellate courts. People displeased with the appellate court's ruling may appeal one more time, to the Supreme Court. The judges on the Supreme Court are called justices.

In order to keep judges independent of any political influence, the Founding Fathers wrote two measures into the Constitution. One defines tenure of office; all federal judges at all three levels serve "during good Behavior;" that is, until they retire, die, or are removed. The purpose of what is basically a lifetime appointment is to free judges from the temptation to decide cases in favor of someone who could vote or do anything else to keep them in office. The second measure is the provision that judges' pay "shall not be diminished during their Continuance in office." This was to remove any worry about the security of their jobs that might influence their decisions.

Setting the number of justices at nine probably also promotes independence. The variety of experience, interests, and reasoning of nine different people makes it unlikely that any one political view will dominate. At times, both Congress and the president have attempted to bolster their power by changing the number, but it has remained at nine since 1869.

O'Connor had difficulty finding a job with her law degree; not many people liked the idea of a female lawyer in 1952. Once she found employment, she, like Thomas, was recognized as a skillful attorney.

Both Thomas and O'Connor worked as state assistant attorneys general, Thomas in Missouri and O'Connor in Arizona. O'Connor had more judiciary experience than Thomas—six years to his sixteen months—but hers was in state courts and his in a federal court. She spent four of her twenty-four years on the federal bench with Thomas. Analysts often classify O'Connor as a moderate conservative, far closer to the center than Thomas.

The other three women with whom Thomas has shared the bench are decidedly liberal. One is Ruth Bader Ginsburg, who joined the high court two years after Thomas. The two judges got to know each other when they served together on the District of Columbia Circuit Court. Ginsburg's passion is correcting gender discrimination, of which she has been a victim. Before becoming a judge, she led the Women's Rights Project of the American Civil Liberties Union and won six important cases in the Supreme Court. She is for gender equity something like what Thurgood Marshall was for racial equality. Despite their differing opinions on many if not most cases, Thomas has called her "a fabulous judge" and "a friend."[1]

Thomas also considers the two women who came to the court after Ginsburg his friends. The first, in 2009, was Sonia Sotomayor. The daughter of native Puerto Ricans, Sotomayor is the first Hispanic on the high court. She came to that position after a thirty-year career in law. She began as an assistant district attorney in New York, prosecuting all kinds of crimes, from petty theft to murder. In private practice, she dealt with business and corporate matters. In her first

The three female justices are pioneers: Elena Kagan (*left*), first female solicitor general; Sonia Sotomayor (*center*), first Hispanic on the court; and Ruth Bader Ginsburg (*right*), first female member of the *Harvard Law Review*.

judgeship, on a US district court in New York, she became somewhat famous as the judge who "saved baseball." Her ruling against team owners and for the players put an end to a threatened strike. As an appellate court judge, she wrote more than 350 majority opinions.

Sotomayor and Thomas had an early experience in common; both entered law school through affirmative action. Like Thomas, Sotomayor also felt the sting of racial bias. A lawyer on campus to hire young talent suggested her grades were not really earned. Unlike Thomas, who seethed inwardly, Sotomayor filed a complaint against the lawyer and received an apology. This victory against prejudice and ignorance revealed what would become her manner of getting to the truth in the courtroom.

When asked about Thomas after working alongside him for nine years, Sotomayor said she admired him and had come to appreciate his views. She pointed out that he was the justice "with whom I probably disagree the most." Yet, she continued, "I just love the man—as a person."[2]

The woman who joined the court a year after Sotomayor, Elena Kagan, has a similar respect for Thomas. Kagan is rare among Supreme Court justices; she had no judicial experience prior to her appointment. She had plenty of experience with the law, not only as a practicing attorney, but also as a law-school professor. She worked as a lawyer for the Senate Judiciary Committee as well as associate counsel for President Bill Clinton. Immediately before being nominated for the position she now holds, she was the first female solicitor general, the lawyer who argues cases in the Supreme Court on behalf of the federal government. Thomas described Kagan as "a delight." Recognizing they are at opposite ends of the left-right spectrum, he welcomed her to the court with a smile and a friendly prediction: "It's going to be a joy disagreeing with you for years to come."[3]

Two Peas in a Pod

While Thomas generally disagreed with the liberal women on the court, he shared most of the judicial perspectives and reasoning of Justice Antonin Scalia. The two men sat together on the bench for a quarter century before Scalia died unexpectedly in 2016. Thomas described Scalia as his closest ally and friend; he said they were like "two peas in a pod."

Thomas's critics at first thought the relationship was lopsided. In the five years before Thomas came to the court, Scalia had established a reputation as a strong conservative and an imposing presence in the courtroom. He asked penetrating questions during oral arguments and did not hesitate to say what he thought of the answers, sometimes in sharp or harsh terms. He disagreed with the majority quite often and appeared to relish tearing apart the statements of the other justices. Thomas, on the other hand, was quiet on the bench. He almost never asked a question or made a comment. And he joined with most of Scalia's opinions. These actions, coupled with Thomas's very brief experience as a judge, prompted some to conclude that he had no mind of his own, that he was being led around by the rather forceful Scalia. They called him Scalia's puppet.

But Thomas's critics did not know what was said behind closed doors, during the judges' conferences. In these gatherings, attended only by the nine justices, Thomas freely stated his opinions, explained his reasoning, and attempted to persuade others. In one of his very first conferences, discussing the case of *Foucha v. Louisiana*, Thomas dissented from, or disagreed with, what all the other judges thought. The justices present their opinions in order of seniority. Because he was the newest justice, Thomas gave his thoughts last. After considering Thomas's points, Scalia changed his vote to agree with Thomas.

Thomas (*left*) said that he and Antonin Scalia (*right*), whom he called "Nino," had an improbable but unbreakable bond of trust and friendship despite their radically different backgrounds.

Chief Justice Rehnquist also changed his mind, as did Justice Kennedy. The case was the first of several in which Thomas, not Scalia, presented the convincing argument.

Off the Court

Friendships and alliances among the justices in the court and conference rooms do not necessarily carry over into the social sphere. While the court is conducting its business, from October to June or July, the justices enjoy many informal times together. However, they do not usually spend leisure time with one another.

One notable exception is Antonin Scalia and Ruth Bader Ginsburg. Friends for over thirty years, they and their spouses always celebrated New Year's Eve together. Their tradition was that Scalia, an avid hunter, supplied the meat and Ginsburg's husband cooked it. The couples took vacations together, and the justices enjoyed each other's company at operas. Once, they actually performed together, appearing as extras in a Washington production of a Strauss opera.

For the most part, however, the justices' interests differ. For example, while Ginsburg loves opera, Thomas prefers bluegrass or jazz. When it comes to sports, Justice Samuel Alito is an avid Philadelphia Phillies fan, but Thomas follows football, specifically the Dallas Cowboys and the Nebraska Cornhuskers. He also loves car races; he is a NASCAR enthusiast and was once grand marshal at the Daytona 500. For exercise, Justice Stephen Breyer rides a bike; Sotomayor likes salsa dancing; and Ginsburg, in her eighties, works out with a personal trainer.

In the summer, Justice Kennedy goes to Austria, where he teaches, and Thomas travels all over the country with his wife in their 40-foot (12 meter) motor home. RVing, he says, is his lifelong passion. He loves meeting ordinary Americans in small towns, RV parks, and Walmart parking lots, where he sometimes spends the night when on the road. He explains, "RVing allows me to get out and see the real America. In RV campgrounds, you wave at everybody, and they wave back. We're all here for the same reason. The best people in the country can be found in RV campgrounds."[4]

Thomas truly loves getting to know "ordinary people." Even his detractors recognize that he is almost universally liked in the Supreme Court building. He talks with everyone—security guards, janitors, servers in the cafeteria—and knows all their names. He has a special relationship with the lawyers who work as his law clerks.

Thomas wants his clerks to understand the history behind the law. How can young people appreciate the importance of the Fourteenth Amendment without knowing its history, including its terrible cost? To impress upon the clerks that the law is not just about the words of a document, but also about the reasons the words were written, Thomas takes them on a field trip every year at the end of the court's session. They visit Gettysburg, one of the bloodiest battlefields of the Civil War. He wants them to see and feel something of why and how the amendment came into being.

The annual trip to Gettysburg reveals something about how Clarence Thomas thinks about the Constitution, of which the Fourteenth Amendment is a part. He has a deep reverence for it. He believes it was written by men who knew firsthand the value and price of freedom. It has stood the test of time and contains mechanisms for correcting its flaws. He believes that its words, penned in another era, are just as applicable today as they were 150 years ago. These beliefs have shaped Thomas's work on the Supreme Court.

CHAPTER FOUR

Making His Mark

T he vast majority of the cases the Supreme Court accepts are appeals. That means someone objected to a decision of a circuit court. The objecting party, called the petitioner, petitions, or asks, the high court to look at the case, listen to its explanation as to why it disagrees with the lower court's ruling, and decide who is right. The petitioner could be a person, a company or organization, or a government body. The other party in the original case, the one that did not ask for the appeal, is called the respondent.

When a case rises through the lower courts all the way to the Supreme Court, the issue usually has to do with a law. A petitioner may claim the respondent did not enforce the law correctly. Or the petitioner may believe

The forty-four marble steps at the entrance to the Supreme Court building tell people this is the highest court in the land. However, the justices can enter through a side door and take an elevator to their chambers.

the law is not valid because it is unconstitutional. Thus the court is a check on both the executive branch of government, which enforces laws, and the legislative branch, which makes laws that must adhere to the Constitution. Those two branches are political; their members are elected and are responsible to the people who elected them. The federal judiciary is not political. Judges are not elected; they are responsible to the Constitution.

Interpreting the Constitution

All the justices firmly believe the Constitution is the final authority on any law. But they do not all have the same perspective on the Constitution. There are two very basic, very different ways of looking at the Constitution: the "living document" approach and the originalist approach.

In the living document perspective, the meaning of the Constitution evolves, or changes, as society changes. In the originalist view, the Constitution means what it meant originally, when it was written. The two perspectives agree that the Constitution itself can be altered only through the amendment process. It is the *meaning* of the words of the Constitution that is at issue in the two approaches. Living-document proponents believe new meanings can emerge as situations arise that were not present or even imagined when the document was written. Originalists believe the Founding Fathers' understanding of the words' meanings should be applied to the new situation.

Take, for example, these words of the Fifth Amendment, known as the "takings clause": "nor shall private property be taken for public use without just compensation." An originalist understands "taken for public use" to mean the government or its citizens actually use the property. A highway or a school would be "public use." A living-document proponent interprets "taken for public use" as using the property for any purpose that benefits the public in some way.

The difference in the two approaches can be seen in the 2005 case of *Kelo v. New London*. In that dispute, a Connecticut city confiscated land from Susette Kelo and

In 2005, Susette Kelo stands on the property she had just lost in a court case. She was able to move her home to another location. Kelo's case caused forty-three states to make laws to prevent similar government actions.

sold it to a company that intended to build new businesses on it. The city reasoned that the jobs the development would bring to the community and the tax revenue it would add to the city constituted public use. This is a living-document argument, and it prevailed in the courts. The originalist dissent, penned by Justice Thomas, countered that because the property was used by neither the government nor the public, its taking was unconstitutional.

Originalism is sometimes called strict constructionism because of its strict adherence to the original meaning. Originalists are usually thought of as conservative because their decisions often result in outcomes that conservatives prefer, such as a reduction in the power of the federal government. People taking the living-document view may be called loose constructionists. Their line of reasoning frequently produces liberal results, primarily greater involvement of the government. Some justices, especially originalists, prefer to call themselves textualists. Textualists focus on the plain, ordinary meaning of the words in the documents they are called upon to interpret.

A Higher Law in the Background

Clarence Thomas is an originalist. His opinions are peppered with the phrase "as originally understood." He accepts that the Constitution is "a modern, 'breathing' document … in the strict sense that the Court is constantly required to interpret how its provisions apply to the Constitutional questions of modern life."[1] But he believes a judge must hold the words of the provisions to mean what the people who wrote them meant at the time they wrote. Sometimes that is easy; much of the document is clear and simple. When the words or phrasing are difficult to decipher, other writings of the founders and

LAW OR JUSTICE?

The nineteenth-century Supreme Court justice Oliver Wendell Holmes Jr. once told a lawyer, "This is a court of law, young man, not a court of justice." That brief quip suggests two distinct views of the judiciary fleshed out in two different methods of reaching decisions: judicial restraint and judicial activism.

Judicial restraint is based on the notion that the role of the judge is simply to rule on whether a law or practice has been written and executed according to the Constitution—nothing more. Judges who practice judicial restraint are concerned only with what the law says, not with whether the law is just or good. They may dislike a particular law because they believe it is not good, but if it is constitutional, they rule in its favor. What is important to them is the separation of the courts from the legislature. They believe if Congress made a bad law, it is Congress that must correct it, not the courts.

By contrast, judicial activists see the role of judges as promoting social welfare. They believe laws should be interpreted and carried out in ways that achieve justice. If they dislike a law because they feel it is not good, they see it as their duty to rule against it. Their concept of what is best for society is their overriding concern. If Congress makes a bad law, the courts must correct it. Judicial activism may be summed up in the words of Thurgood Marshall: "You do what you think is right and let the law catch up."

their contemporaries can be used to help explain the text. But what if the meaning is still uncertain? Thomas's answer is to examine the text in light of natural law—equality and possession of certain human rights.

This is the somewhat unique perspective Thomas brings to originalism. It is where he differs from late justice Antonin Scalia and other outspoken originalists. Thomas believes the Constitution is rooted in the principles of natural law as expressed in the Declaration of Independence. Those principles are the "self-evident truths" that "all men are created equal, that they are endowed by their Creator with certain unalienable Rights." This statement, he says, is "natural law in a nutshell."[2] Unalienable rights are rights that people have simply because they are people. These rights belong to "all men" with or without a Constitution, so the Constitution does not *give* anyone any rights; it merely protects them.

Thomas sees natural law as the background of the Constitution.

The US Constitution, Declaration of Independence, and Bill of Rights are the primary documents upon which Thomas bases his understanding of original intent. He supplements these with the Federalist Papers and other writings of the Founding Fathers.

It is a higher law, accepted as such by the Founding Fathers. The Constitution created a structure for protecting the unalienable rights of the higher law. Thomas does not base his judicial opinions on natural law. Rather, he uses natural law to provide a deeper understanding of Constitutional provisions.

Natural Law and Constitutional Law

One example that illustrates Thomas's understanding is the 2010 case of *McDonald v. Chicago*. The issue in that case was whether states could make laws banning guns. The Second Amendment to the Constitution clearly states, "The right of the people to keep and bear Arms shall not be infringed." The City of Chicago argued that the Constitution is a federal document, defining primarily what the federal government can and cannot do; it should not affect states unless it specifically mentions them. Therefore, although the federal government could not infringe on, or violate, someone's right to have a gun, the state of Illinois could.

Four of the justices agreed with the city. Four others applied the Fourteenth Amendment's "due process" clause: "No state shall … deprive any person of life, liberty, or property, without due process of law." They interpreted this to mean that states could not deprive their citizens of any of the rights in the Bill of Rights, the first ten constitutional amendments. Therefore, these four said, the law was not constitutional.

Thomas also considered Chicago's law unconstitutional, but for a different reason. Looking through the prism of natural law, he believed the Founding Fathers saw bearing arms as an unalienable right, a privilege of self-protection belonging to all citizens by virtue of being human. When justices agree with the decision of the majority on the court but disagree with the reasoning or some other important aspect of the decision, they write concurring opinions.

In his concurrence, Thomas cited the Fourteenth Amendment's "privileges and immunities" clause: "No state shall make or enforce any law which shall abridge the privileges or immunities of citizens of the United States." He pointed out that the term "privileges and immunities," as originally understood, meant rights, and in this case referred to the right to have a gun. He argued that the law in question was clearly unconstitutional; no state could make any law abridging, or cutting short, the unalienable rights of any citizen.

Limiting the Power of Government

Thomas's fifty-six-page concurrence in *McDonald v. Chicago* indicates one of his major concerns. As an originalist, he wants to maintain constitutional limits on government power, especially the power of the federal government. The case, which pitted federal authority against state authority, gave him the opportunity to spell out the importance to him of limited government. He wrote:

> Our system of government rests on one overriding principle: All power stems from the consent of the people. ... The ultimate source of the Constitution's authority is the consent of the people of each individual State, not the consent of the undifferentiated people of the Nation as a whole [that is, of the federal government].[3]

In other cases, he has criticized the courts' use of the due process clause to widen the power of the federal government.

He disagrees with decisions that give federal agencies authority over matters such as private contracts, health care, and minimum wages. He believes any laws about such issues should be created by the states. He also objects to the government using the due process clause to protect what some people believe are rights but that are not listed in the Constitution, such as a right to privacy.

Thomas has challenged another interpretation that has given broad powers to the federal government. That interpretation has to do with the commerce clause. The commerce clause is part of Article I of the Constitution, the article that describes Congress. Section 8 of that article lists a number of tasks Congress is authorized to perform. The items listed are called "enumerated powers" because they are specified, named one after another, like numbers. The commerce clause gives Congress the power "to regulate commerce with foreign nations, and among the several states, and with the Indian tribes."

This power appears rather limited: Congress can make laws about trade with other countries and across state lines. Actually, Congress has expanded that authority from regulating interstate commerce to controlling anything even remotely affecting interstate commerce. By the time Thomas came to the court, the commerce clause was used to justify federal regulation of farming, manufacturing, retail, labor, carbon dioxide emissions, health care, and a host of other concerns. For decades, it seemed to be the go-to rationalization any time Congress wanted to regulate something. The "something" did not even have to be economic; the Civil Rights Act of 1964 was passed under the authority of the commerce clause.

Cases involving the commerce clause had been challenged in the Supreme Court a number of times. However, since 1937, no case involving the clause had been overturned. That changed with *United States v. Lopez* in 1995.

The disputed law in that case was the Gun-Free School Zones Act of 1990. Alfonzo Lopez, a twelfth grader, had brought a gun into his school, as was allowed in Texas but illegal under the federal statute. Lopez argued the federal law went beyond Congress's authority because possessing a gun is not an economic activity. Ruling against a commerce clause regulation for the first time in fifty-eight years, the court found in a 5–4 decision that gun possession has no "substantial effect" on interstate commerce.

The balance scale is often used as a symbol for justice. The idea is that each side in a dispute puts its evidence in one of the pans of the scale. The evidence, and only the evidence, is weighed. Justice is determined by the pan with the greater weight.

Thomas agreed wholeheartedly. He took the ruling as an opportunity to point out the danger he saw in what he considered Congress's stretching of the commerce clause. In his concurrence, he first noted how the courts had interpreted the constitutional provision for almost sixty years: "We [meaning the majority] have said that Congress may regulate not only 'Commerce … among the several states,' but also anything that has a 'substantial effect' on such commerce." Then he explained in detail what he believed was wrong with that interpretation, ending with: "This test, if taken to its logical extreme, would give Congress a 'police power' over all aspects of American life."[4]

Five years later, the Supreme Court followed the precedent it established in *United States v. Lopez*, declaring the Violence Against Women Act of 1994 in violation of the commerce clause. The law was unconstitutional because it allowed the federal government to regulate something that had nothing to do with commerce. In that case, *United States v. Morrison*, Thomas wrote a one-paragraph concurrence simply to remind the justices that they had not dealt with his concern about the proper interpretation of the commerce clause.

That concern resurfaced in 2005 with *Gonzales v. Raich*. At issue was the Controlled Substances Act, a federal law that criminalized possession of marijuana. The government had seized and destroyed marijuana from two women who had grown it at their homes for medicinal use, legal under California law. The court decided 6–3 that the Controlled Substances Act did not exceed Congress's authority under the commerce clause because, even though the women did not sell the plants, growing marijuana is an economic activity. Thomas issued a dissent, the formal explanation of a justice who does not agree with the majority. He again warned of the dangers of what he viewed as a faulty interpretation of a constitutional provision:

> [The parties in the case] use marijuana that has never been bought or sold, that has never crossed state lines, and that has had no demonstrable effect on the national market for marijuana. If Congress can regulate this under the Commerce Clause, then it can regulate virtually anything—and the Federal Government is no longer one of limited and enumerated powers.[5]

Affirmative Action

The question on the court of the reach of federal power brought Thomas face-to-face with a sore subject: affirmative action. He had long believed the government policy of preferential treatment was harmful to those it was intended to benefit. As an originalist, he believed the practice was not constitutional. As a judge, he would have to examine its use.

His first chance to look at affirmative action as a Supreme Court justice came in 1995 in the case of *Adarand Constructors v. Peña*. The case involved companies the government certified as socially and economically disadvantaged. People doing business with the government received financial incentives for employing disadvantaged companies. The government assumed that any minority was disadvantaged; it therefore certified minority-owned companies as disadvantaged. The petitioner in the case claimed this was unfair treatment. The court agreed the government should not classify a company as disadvantaged, and therefore give it preferential treatment, simply on the basis of its owner's race. The 5–4 decision did not strike down affirmative action, but it did disallow it in this case.

The argument of the dissenting justices was the one Thomas had heard for years: because minorities had been treated unfairly in the past, the government needed to correct the injustice by mandating that they be given special considerations. Although the dissent did not change what for Thomas was a victory, he felt he needed to get his opposition to this view into the record. This line of reasoning, he argued, violated the natural law principle behind the equal protection clause of the Fourteenth Amendment. In his concurrence, he wrote:

> I believe that there is a "moral [and] constitutional equivalence" … between laws designed to subjugate a race and those that distribute benefits on the basis of race in order to foster some current notion of equality. Government cannot make us equal; it can only recognize, respect, and protect us as equal before the law.[6]

The subject of affirmative action came before the high court again, in 2003, in the case of *Grutter v. Bollinger*. The petitioner, who was white, had been denied admission to the University of Michigan's law school because of the school's policy of giving preference to blacks. The court ruled that the policy did not violate the equal protection clause because, although race was a major factor in deciding who would be admitted to the school, it was not the only factor. This time, Thomas's dissent was long and impassioned. He not only repeated his constitutional argument regarding the equal protection clause, but he also presented statistics to bolster his contention that policies of racial preference harmed African Americans and others.

In the years that followed, other cases have arisen that have challenged Thomas's position on affirmative action, equal protection, and the overreach of the federal government. In all of them, he has remained unwavering, expressing the same opinions, offering the same arguments, and sticking with the same judicial philosophy. Both his admirers and his critics agree that for his nearly thirty years on the Supreme Court, Clarence Thomas has been absolutely consistent.

CHAPTER FIVE

The Power of Dissent

S upreme Court watchers know Clarence Thomas as the most agreeable and the least agreeing justice. Nearly everyone he has worked with, and all the employees in the Supreme Court building, genuinely like him. However, he disagrees with his colleagues probably more often than any other justice. Every year, he has the record for the most dissents and concurrences (which express some form of disagreement with a majority decision). He authors twice as many as anyone else. Why does Thomas write so many dissents?

Thomas with his wife, Virginia. When Thomas married Virginia Lamp in 1987, she was working as a lobbyist for the US Chamber of Commerce. Thomas's fourteen-year-old son, Jamal, was his best man.

Explaining and Influencing

Thomas dissents so much because he often disagrees with the way the majority decisions are reached. Even though some of the other justices are originalists, Thomas's stubborn adherence to his strict brand of that philosophy makes his reasoning unique. He writes to explain how and why he arrives at the opinions he holds.

Sincere and reasonable people can look at the same facts and come to different conclusions. Cases are often complex, and judges rely on more than one factor in analyzing them. Decisions of the lower courts, precedent, and opinions from similar cases are all considered. Justices weigh the points presented by petitioners and respondents, as well as the likely impact of their rulings on future disputes. They may differ on which factors should be given the greatest weight. Thomas believes the way the justices think through these matters is as important as the conclusions they reach because it tells how they relate the centuries-old Constitution to modern circumstances.

Applying the Constitution faithfully is of utmost concern for all Supreme Court justices. Thomas believes it is important for citizens to know what rights they have and to see exactly how the founding documents continue to safeguard those rights. He has said, "I think we are obligated to make the Constitution, and what we write about the Constitution, accessible to our fellow citizens ... We owe it to people to present to them their Constitution in a way they can understand."[1] Thomas works at his writing, trying to put the sometimes difficult concepts into easily grasped language. He tells his law clerks, who write some of the first drafts and edit later copies, that written opinions should be intelligible to gas station attendants as well as lawyers.

Thomas writes for three audiences: ordinary Americans, lawyers who might study his opinions and adopt some of his reasoning, and other justices who might be persuaded by his arguments. He believes that if contrary viewpoints are important, expressing them rather than remaining silent stimulates healthy dialogue that generates constructive ideas. The discussion forces people to consider perspectives other than their own. It sharpens their thinking about critical issues. It may make them more certain of their convictions, or it may move them in new directions. Sometimes, as in the *Foucha v. Louisiana* case, the dissent changes justices' minds.

A Model for Dissent

One of the greatest values of the written dissent is its potential for the future. Every dissent and every concurrence is part of the official record of the Supreme Court's ruling. When lawyers and judges deal with a case, they research the arguments in similar cases that were decided in the past. The dissent in those cases is in the record for them to consider. They may cite the dissenting opinion as evidence that some justice agrees with them. That citation adds weight to their argument. Over the course of time, the same dissent may appear in more cases. Multiple versions of the same dissent by different justices in a number of cases may eventually result in acceptance of the dissent as a valid argument. Thus a divergent opinion that is little regarded at the time it is written may have a significant impact five, ten, or one hundred years later.

Thomas holds up John Marshall Harlan as an example of the importance and power of dissent. Harlan was an associate justice on the court that decided *Plessy v. Ferguson* in 1896, the ruling that established "separate but equal" as constitutional.

All the justices with the exception of Harlan signed on to the majority opinion. Harlan penned a remarkably strong dissent that is still quoted today in civil rights cases. It directly refuted the court's decision:

> In the view of the Constitution, in the eye of the law, there is in this country no superior, dominant, ruling class of citizens. There is no caste here. Our Constitution is color-blind and neither knows nor tolerates classes among citizens. In respect of civil rights, all citizens are equal before the law. The humblest is the peer of the most powerful. The law regards man as man and takes no account of his surroundings or of his color when his civil rights as guaranteed by the supreme law of the land are involved.[2]

Despite the wisdom of Harlan's words, *Plessy v. Ferguson* remained unchallenged for almost sixty years. But the dissent was not forgotten. It was on record, and Thurgood Marshall cited it as he argued the case of *Brown v. Board of Education*, which overturned the *Plessy* decision.

When he speaks to groups, Thomas frequently asks his audiences what would have happened if Harlan had not written his dissent. It was unpopular at the time, and he was harshly ridiculed. Is being alone in an opinion reason to stay silent? Harlan's contemporaries criticized him because his thinking was not in the mainstream. Thomas asks, "Does that make him wrong? Who was right? The Court? The majority? Or the dissent? What if there were no dissent by Harlan? … Maybe it didn't persuade his colleagues, but it persuaded history."[3]

On the steps of the Supreme Court building, the three attorneys who argued and won the *Brown v. Board of Education of Topeka, Kansas* case: (*from left to right*) George E.C. Hayes, Thurgood Marshall, and James Nabrit Jr.

MAKING UP THEIR MINDS

Supreme Court procedures are very regimented. Each year's session opens the first Monday in October. Cases are heard through April on Mondays, Tuesdays, and Wednesdays at precisely 10:00 a.m. The justices meet at 10:00 a.m. on Mondays in May and June to announce their major rulings. They recess, or take a break, in late June or early July.

The Supreme Court accepts about eighty of the approximately seven thousand requests for a hearing it receives each year. Once a case is put on the court's docket, or schedule, the petitioner submits a brief. The brief is a written statement, in fifty or fewer pages, outlining the petitioner's arguments. The respondent then presents its brief, also limited to fifty pages. If other parties want to express their opinions about the case, they may also submit briefs.

The justices read the briefs prior to the court date. They typically hear two cases on each court date, limiting each to an hour. Parties are given thirty minutes each to present their oral arguments. The justices may ask questions to get a better understanding of the parties' positions, but the questioning is part of the thirty-minute time limit. If the government does not play a part in the case but has a relevant point to make, an additional thirty minutes may be allotted to a government lawyer.

Justices meet in conference on Wednesday and Friday afternoons. They discuss the week's cases and cast their votes, beginning with the chief justice and proceeding according to seniority, from the most veteran justice to the newest. If one side receives a majority of votes, a justice is assigned to write the majority's opinion. Other justices may write concurring or dissenting opinions if they choose. However, this is not the final word.

The gavel is a symbol of judgment and order in a courtroom. Supreme Court justices have strict schedules and depend on order to make decisions.

For an opinion to become the court's opinion, a majority of the justices must agree to all its parts and formally "sign on" to it. Drafts of all the written opinions are circulated among all the justices. Sometimes the well-thought-out and carefully worded drafts raise additional questions or offer fresh insights. New drafts are written, opinions evolve, and votes are sometimes changed. On occasion, what began as a dissent ends up as the majority opinion.

Petitioners or respondents may disagree with the court's ruling, but none can contest the fact that their case was handled seriously, thoroughly, and according to well-established protocols.

Persuading History

When Thomas dissents, he writes for the same reason Harlan did: to persuade history. He knows that many consider his views too conservative to be in the mainstream. However, like Harlan, he believes they are right, and he hopes they will eventually be accepted. So he continues to painstakingly explain what he sees as the original intent of various constitutional concepts. And he asks his fellow justices to reconsider the ways they interpret the provisions.

He does this primarily in his concurring opinions. For example, in his concurrence in the *United States v. Lopez* gun case, Thomas detailed the meaning and history of the commerce clause in order "to show how far we have departed from the original understanding." He suggested, "In a future case, we ought to temper our Commerce Clause jurisprudence in a manner that … is more faithful to the original understanding of that Clause."[4]

Similarly, in *McDonald v. Chicago*, after a lengthy discussion of the Fourteenth Amendment's privileges and immunities and due process clauses, Thomas suggested, "This case presents an opportunity to reexamine, and begin the process of restoring, the meaning of the Fourteenth Amendment agreed upon by those who ratified it."[5] In other concurrences, he called upon the justices, as well as future justices, to reconsider rulings regarding the definition of cruel and unusual punishment, the takings clause, the limits on free speech, and other constitutional issues.

Issues of Race

Thomas's desire to persuade people to his interpretation of the Fourteenth Amendment has earned him some detractors. Many African Americans who had hoped Thurgood Marshall's replacement would champion their view of civil rights have been disappointed in Thomas's pronouncements from the bench. They were unhappy with the opposition to affirmative action he voiced in *Adarand Constructors v. Peña* and *Grutter v. Bollinger*. He repeated that opposition in 2012 in his concurrence in *Fisher v. University of Texas*.

The critics were equally upset with Thomas's opinions in *Northwest Austin Municipal Utility District No. 1 v. Holder* in 2009 and *Shelby County v. Holder* in 2013. These cases dealt with the Voting Rights Act of 1965, which prohibited racial discrimination at the ballot box. The law was a hard-won triumph of the civil rights movement and had done much to protect the voting rights of African Americans, particularly in the South. It has long been recognized as one of the most important and effective laws in modern American history. At issue in both cases was a section of the act affecting states with a history of suppressing the black vote. According to the provision, voting districts in those states could not change anything about their election requirements unless they received authorization from the Department of Justice.

In both cases, some problems were found with the legislation, but the core elements were retained. Thomas agreed with both judgments that kept the Voting Rights Act in place, but in his concurrences, he stated that he believed the section in question was not constitutional. Civil rights advocates were concerned that if other justices followed Thomas, they could lose one of the most important safeguards of their right to vote.

Reexamining the Past

African Americans are not the only ones critical of Thomas. His repeated call for the court to reassess past decisions has

President Lyndon Johnson (*seated*) signs the Voting Rights Act of 1965 as Martin Luther King Jr. (*fifth from right*), Rosa Parks (*third from right*), and other civil rights activists look on. The law has been amended five times to make it stronger.

worried many in the legal community. They see it as toying with a principle judges have long followed in their analyses of law, the concept of *stare decisis*. The name comes from the first words of the Latin motto "*stare decisis et non quieta movere*," meaning "stand by what is decided and do not disturb what is settled." In short, *stare decisis* means making legal decisions on the basis of previous decisions. Once a ruling is made about a particular act—whether it is legal and, if not, what penalty should be imposed—that ruling becomes a precedent. The next time a similar action is brought to a judge, the judge delivers the same ruling as the preceding judge.

The concept of *stare decisis* was part of common law, the unwritten legal code America inherited from England. It is not in the Constitution or any of the other early documents. Yet it has been an important principle of American jurisprudence, its legal system, since the nation's founding. In the Supreme Court's early days, justices frequently cited the precedents of English common law to guide their decisions. Gradually, the court developed its own set of rulings that serve as precedents today.

When a number of precedents that all say the same thing have been built up, the result is called case law. Case law is not the same as statutory laws, which are the laws passed by Congress and state legislatures. However, the decisions of the Supreme Court—that is, case law—are just as binding as laws passed by Congress. When enough precedent has been built up, *stare decisis* takes effect and the matter is considered "settled law."

Stare decisis brings four benefits to courts that the Constitution alone cannot provide: stability, fairness, legitimacy, and efficiency. Looking to past decisions gives stability to the system by making results predictable. Citizens know what to expect from the courts. Treating similar cases alike gives people

When a person is arrested, as in this photo, the arresting officer must inform the person of four specific rights, called Miranda rights. This requirement is case law; it arose from the 1966 Supreme Court decision in *Miranda v. Arizona*.

confidence that the system is fair. It keeps judges from making up arbitrary rules. Having a solid foundation for decisions gives the sense that the system is legitimate, established on justice, operating according to laws. Finally, *stare decisis* is efficient; using precedents frees judges from the burden of beginning the arguments for every case from square one.

However, *stare decisis* has drawbacks too. Relying on the same reasoning for the same matters can blind judges to other ways of seeing an issue. It can become a general rule, an easy answer that keeps judges from examining the nuances of a specific case. What if an original precedent was a bad ruling? *Stare decisis* hardens it into settled law, making it very difficult to change.

But bad decisions can be changed. *Brown v. Board of Education* overturned *Plessy v. Ferguson*. *United States v. Lopez* changed the rules about the commerce clause. Settled law can be unsettled. *Stare decisis* is a valuable tool, but it is not any more binding than a statutory law that is repealed.

Justice Thomas acknowledged "the importance of *stare decisis* to the stability of our Nation's legal system. But," he reminded the other justices, "*stare decisis* is only an 'adjunct' [that is, an extra help] of our duty as judges to decide by our best lights what the Constitution means."[6] For Thomas, the originalist, everything takes second place to the Constitution, included settled law. He believes "the Constitution itself, the written document, is the ultimate *stare decisis*."[7]

A Looming Controversy

The people who fear Thomas may be willing to challenge decisions they think are firm are right to worry. He has stated repeatedly that if a case was wrongly settled, it should be reexamined not in light of precedent, but in accordance with the Constitution. The matter that appears to be of greatest concern to many people is *Roe v. Wade*, the 1973 decision that recognized a woman's right to an abortion.

In that case, often simply called *Roe*, the Supreme Court ruled that the right to terminate a pregnancy was part of the

Norma McCovey (*left*), known as Jane Roe in *Roe v Wade*, and attorney Gloria Allred (*right*) make a statement as the Supreme Court considers a challenge to *Roe v. Wade* in 1989.

right to privacy. The right to privacy had been established eight years earlier in another case. Actually, the 1973 decision focused on the privacy of doctors who performed abortions more than on the privacy of the women who had them. Nevertheless, it invalidated laws of forty-six states that had prohibited abortions. States could place some restrictions on the practice of abortion, but they could not deny women what was now their right to terminate their pregnancies. The ruling was given twenty years before Thomas came to the court.

Over those twenty years, more than ten Supreme Court decisions clarified and refined the basic tenets of *Roe* and reaffirmed its acceptance. This case law enabled people to call the decision settled law. However, to those opposed to abortion, it was not settled.

In 1992, people challenged some restrictions Pennsylvania had placed on receiving an abortion. In that case, *Planned Parenthood v. Casey*, the court upheld *Roe* while also ruling in favor of most of the Pennsylvania restrictions being challenged.

Casey was decided during Thomas's second year on the bench. Instead of writing his own dissent, he joined with Scalia in saying, "The States may, if they wish, permit abortion on demand, but the Constitution does not *require* them to do so." Perhaps more importantly, he also joined with Rehnquist's dissent: "We believe that *Roe* was wrongly decided, and that it can and should be overruled."[8]

If that was not enough to send shivers down the backs of abortion supporters, Thomas's two-sentence concurrence in *Gonzales v. Carhart*, a 2007 ruling that upheld a ban on partial-birth abortion, troubled them. He said, "I write separately to reiterate my view that the Court's abortion jurisprudence, including *Casey* and *Roe v. Wade*, … has no basis in the Constitution."[9]

Thomas is not a crusader. He is not on a mission to overturn specific precedents. He is not an activist determined to see his ideas on racial matters carried out. He is a judge who understands that his duty is "to interpret and apply the choices made in [the legislative and executive] branches, not to make policy choices."[10] Because he is committed to his oath to "administer justice without respect to persons," he is not concerned with how popular he is with any one group. His goal is simply to see the laws and practices of the United States line up with the Constitution … as originally understood. His dogged pursuit of that goal has won him numerous admirers and probably an equal number of critics.

CHAPTER SIX

A Quiet Legacy

O n February 29, 2016, Clarence Thomas stunned everyone when he posed a question to an attorney presenting her case. The question itself was not surprising; it was about the connection of the argument to a constitutional right—just the type of subject that always interested the justice. What amazed the observers in the courtroom was that he asked a question at all. It was the first time he had done so in ten years.

Thomas's reputation for silence on the bench is legendary. The other justices ask so many questions they sometimes interrupt one another. However, Thomas rarely speaks. He explains that each lawyer has only

Justices Anthony Kennedy (*left*), Clarence Thomas (*center*), and John Roberts (*right*) at the 2017 presidential inauguration. The justices wear their robes at all official functions.

thirty minutes, and he feels it is rude and unproductive to take their time with his questions. He is there to hear the lawyers' perspectives, and he can learn best by listening. But although he has little to say during oral arguments, he has much to say in his written opinions. Thomas's legacy is not in his speaking, but in his writing.

Winning the Long Game

Much of that writing, especially in the first half of Thomas's Supreme Court tenure, expressed ideas with which few, if any, of his colleagues agreed. Even Justice Antonin Scalia, who shared Thomas's originalist philosophy and his conservative leaning, could not sign on to some of his opinions. Often Thomas was alone in his dissents. He took comfort in the example of Justice Harlan, whose dissent in *Plessy* became the majority opinion sixty years later and remains so today. Like Harlan, Thomas is playing the long game, trusting that history will eventually prove him right.

Today, after many years and many dissents, his impact is being felt. Thomas's first fourteen years on the bench were on what was called the Rehnquist court, named after the chief justice for that period. That court tended liberal, so much of what Thomas wrote fell on deaf ears. Justice Scalia made sure the conservative perspective was presented, and he too was often ignored. But Scalia was a large presence, assertive in oral arguments and colorful in his written opinions, so the quieter Thomas was frequently in his shadow. For that reason, Thomas was often depicted in the press as intellectually empty, a man with no ideas of his own, a judge of no consequence.

However, that depiction was far from the truth. The general public may have known only that Thomas disagreed a lot. They

Chief Justice John Roberts (*far right*) congratulates Samuel Alito (*left, shaking hands*) after swearing him in as associate justice on February 1, 2006. President George W. Bush (*far left*), who appointed both men to the court, and Alito's family look on.

were not aware that his dissents were clear and persuasive, based on reasoned arguments. They were discussed seriously in conferences, and they chipped away, little by little, at opposing views. Many of Thomas's opinions rejected on the Rehnquist court became law on the Roberts court.

The appointment of John Roberts as chief justice in 2005, and of Samuel Alito as associate justice the next year, added two conservative justices to the court. Their thinking was more closely aligned with Thomas's. The decisions of the Roberts court began to incorporate some of Thomas's philosophy. Even justices who describe themselves as living-document proponents began paying more attention to original intent. Justice Elena Kagan, in a 2015 appearance at Harvard Law School, told her audience, "We're all textualists now."[1]

Recognition

Some of Thomas's harshest critics who once wrote him off as intellectually bankrupt and a blind follower of Scalia have admitted that he is not only brilliant but also a leader. Jeffrey Toobin, journalist and legal analyst for CNN and *New Yorker* magazine, has followed Thomas's career since before he came to the Supreme Court. He disagrees with nearly all of Thomas's court opinions and has written harsh critiques of his performance, yet he has recognized that Thomas, by his consistent clinging to what he believes is right, has built a legacy. He observed in 2011:

> Since the arrival of Chief Justice John Roberts in 2005, and Justice Samuel Alito in 2006, the court has moved to the right when it comes to the free-speech rights of corporations, the rights of gun owners, and potentially, the powers of the federal government; in each of these areas, the majority has followed where Thomas has been leading for a decade or more. Rarely has a Supreme Court justice enjoyed such broad or significant vindication.[2]

Another critic, Thomas Goldstein, a liberal attorney who founded SCOTUSblog, a widely read blog that follows the Supreme Court (SCOTUS is an acronym for "Supreme Court of the United States"), has said much the same thing. Although not by any means a fan of the justice, his statement captures the reasons Thomas will have a lasting impact on the country:

> I disagree profoundly with Justice Thomas's views on many questions, but if you believe that Supreme

Court decision-making should be a contest of ideas rather than power, so that the measure of a justice's greatness is his contribution to new and thoughtful perspectives that enlarge the debate, then Justice Thomas is now our greatest justice.[3]

If Goldstein is correct, Thomas's legacy will be bigger than his ideas. It will be more than any persuasion to originalism or

Gregory Maggs asks Thomas about his autobiography during a 2018 lecture. A former Thomas law clerk, Maggs was a colonel in the army, a law school professor, and was appointed judge on the US Court of Appeals for the Armed Forces in 2018.

UNSUNG HEROES

In a single year, the nine Supreme Court justices must sort through seven thousand requests for a hearing, read and digest a minimum of eight thousand pages of briefs, recall decades of cases and opinions, and consider and write lengthy decisions. All of this is in addition to overseeing the thirteen circuit courts. How do they manage the overwhelming workload? They rely heavily on their law clerks.

The clerks divide up the thousands of applications for hearings, called "writs of *certiorari*," or "certs" for short. They condense them into memos, adding their recommendations for or against accepting the case. The justices, relieved of the burden of wading through long arguments, often read only the memos when deciding which cases to accept.

Once a cert has been granted and the justices have read the briefs, they discuss the case with their clerks. The clerks are fairly new lawyers, but they have some experience, and the justices value their perspectives. Besides, most justices use this exercise as an opportunity to develop their clerks, helping them grow professionally. Under the guidance of the justices, the law clerks research laws and precedents, helping the justices prepare to hear the case. After oral arguments, the clerks may write first drafts of the justices' opinions.

Each justice has four clerks, and the chief justice can have five. They generally serve for one or two years. Clerking on the Supreme Court can be a stepping stone to other, more prestigious positions. Of people who were once Supreme Court law clerks, eight have become Supreme Court justices. The job may be unsung, but it has its benefits.

the adoption of some opinion. It will go beyond influencing people to conservative or liberal thinking. Thomas's legacy may very well be the fact that his "thoughtful perspectives," no matter how extreme they appear to some, have "enlarged the debate" about issues that matter.

Neomi Rao, a former Thomas law clerk, was appointed administrator for the White House Office of Information and Regulatory Affairs in 2017. It is a powerful position, overseeing the regulations proposed or imposed by federal departments and agencies.

A Living Legacy

Clarence Thomas's legacy will be deep because his influence has been wide. In his more than twenty-five years on the bench, Thomas has had more than one hundred law clerks. He treats them like family, like his children, and they return his affection and respect. He has lunch with them about once a month, and not just the four working for him at the time. Many former clerks join them if they are in Washington; sometimes, they need a table for twenty.

Thomas hires as his clerks lawyers who share his judicial philosophy, and he talks with them about how he sees the law and the Constitution. As he discusses cases with them, they learn his methods of reasoning. During his tenure, Thomas has trained an army of some of the brightest men and women in America. These former law clerks, some now in their fifties, are multiplying their mentor's influence.

Many are teaching in law schools from Virginia to California and points between. Thomas has said that law schools in the 1970s concentrated on statutory and case law, giving little attention to constitutional law. His clerks, now professors and lecturers, are producing a generation of lawyers schooled in the principles of original intent.

Some former Thomas clerks are in private practice, and others are working for corporations or nonprofit groups. At least twenty-two have positions in the federal government. Four have high-level jobs in federal agencies; two are assistant secretaries of the Treasury Department, one is General Counsel of the Department of Transportation, and one heads the Office of Information and Regulatory Affairs, concerned with government regulations. Thomas has been outspoken in his opinions about government regulations.

Several of Thomas's former clerks are federal lawyers. Some have served on the White House legal team, one is the top federal prosecutor in Kansas, and one is the principal deputy solicitor general.

Four of Thomas's former clerks have become judges on the circuit courts. They are located across the country, on courts in Washington DC, Denver, Saint Louis, and New Orleans. These are potential positions of great influence, and that influence is part of Thomas's legacy.

After clerking for Thomas, Laura Ingraham practiced in a law firm before launching a career as a radio and television talk-show host. Here she is speaking at the 2016 Republican National Convention.

A Personal Legacy

Another part is his personal story. Thomas's life, like his career, has had its ups and downs. And also like his career, the second half has vindicated the first; he has been able to turn around all the "downs." Thomas would not list growing up in the segregated South as one of the negatives despite some unpleasant incidents. He considers his upbringing in a typical black home with solid, traditional values one of the blessings of his life. The dark spots he would name would be those of his own making: the anger that nearly consumed him as a young man, the struggle with alcohol, the decision to leave his first wife. If he were cataloging the negatives, he would probably include the mountain of debt he accumulated in his quest for the best education. He was still paying off his student loans when he joined the Supreme Court, seventeen years after earning his degree! Of course, his confirmation process was another monumental low.

However, Thomas overcame all those obstacles. In his career, it was his consistency, his refusal to veer from what he considered right, that was the key to coming out on top. So, too, in his personal struggles, it was his refusal to give up that brought him success. It was clinging to his grandfather's words: "Old Man Can't is dead." He conquered his anger, stopped drinking, and paid his debt a little at a time. He remarried, but he also mended his relationship with his first wife, and they raised their son together.

In his personal story, Thomas is carrying on a legacy that was bequeathed to him. His grandfather had told him that learning to work hard would be his inheritance. He certainly learned that lesson, and he passed it on to the next generation, his son and his law clerks. He received other gifts from his grandfather: a love for learning, a reverence for God, the importance of

Thomas has become a popular speaker for college commencements, university lecture series, attorneys' groups, and various organizations, including the Recreational Vehicle Industry Association. Here he addresses the 2007 National Lawyers Convention.

discipline, the commitment to do what is right. These, too, he is passing on to those who will come after him.

In many ways, Thomas is like his grandfather. Just as Myers Anderson took in little Clarence as a young child and raised him as his own, Thomas adopted his six-year-old great-nephew in 1997. He instilled in him the same values and lessons his grandfather imparted to him.

In both the legal field and his personal life, Clarence Thomas is doing things that make a difference now and in the future. He is impacting people who will, in turn, impact others. That is his legacy. His grandfather—his hero, the person he calls the greatest man he has ever known—would be proud of him.

CHRONOLOGY

1896 *Plessy v. Ferguson* decision legalizes "separate but equal" policy; Justice John Marshall Harlan dissents.

1948 Clarence Thomas is born in Pin Point, Georgia.

1954 *Brown v. Board of Education* decision declares "separate but equal" doctrine unconstitutional.

1955 Thomas and his brother begin living with their grandparents, Myers and Christine Anderson, in Savannah, Georgia, as their children.

1964–1968 Thomas attends St. John Vianney Minor Seminary in Savannah and Conception Seminary College in Conception, Missouri, both all-black schools.

1968 Martin Luther King Jr. is shot and killed.

1968–1971 Thomas completes his junior and senior years at the predominantly white College of the Holy Cross in Worcester, Massachusetts, graduating cum laude.

1971–1974 Thomas attends Yale Law School, graduating with a JD (doctor of jurisprudence) degree.

1971 Thomas marries Kathy Grace Ambush; they separate in 1981 and divorce in 1984.

1973 Jamal Thomas is born to Clarence and Kathy Thomas.

1974–1977 Thomas serves as assistant attorney general of Missouri under John Danforth.

1979–1990 Thomas works in Washington, DC, first as legislative assistant to US Senator John Danforth, then as assistant secretary for civil rights in the Department of Education, and then as chairman of the US Equal Employment Opportunity Commission.

1987 Thomas marries Virginia Lamp.

1990–1991 Thomas serves sixteen months as a judge on the US Court of Appeals for the District of Columbia circuit.

1991 After a difficult confirmation process, Thomas becomes an associate Supreme Court justice.

1995 Thomas concurs in *United States v. Lopez*, a case that limited federal power under the commerce clause.

2010 Thomas's concurrence in *McDonald v. City of Chicago* presents his understanding of the "privileges and immunities" clause of the Fourteenth Amendment.

2003 Thomas dissents in *Grutter v. Bollinger*, a case that upheld affirmative action.

2016 Associate Justice Antonin Scalia dies, and Thomas becomes the leading conservative on the Supreme Court.

GLOSSARY

affirmative action The policy begun in 1960 of giving favored treatment in hiring and school admissions to minorities who had historically suffered from discrimination.

appellate court A federal court that hears and rules on cases that have been settled in a lower, district court when the losing party in the lower court case asks for a higher court to review the case.

Black Codes Laws enacted by Southern states after emancipation to severely restrict the freedoms of newly emancipated African Americans.

brief A written document provided by one party in a legal action giving the legal grounds for the action and the reasons the party believes it should prevail.

case law Laws that are formed from the precedents, or judgments in cases, of the courts rather than from legislation.

certiorari Latin for "to be informed of," this is the process of ordering a lower court to submit records to a higher court that will inform the higher court of the facts of a case. It is basically an application to a court to hear an appeal.

color line The term for the separation of blacks from whites.

concurrence A judge's written opinion agreeing with the decision of the majority but disagreeing with the reasoning for the decision.

cum laude Latin for "with honor" or "with distinction." It is an honor usually given to graduates who earn a grade point average of about 3.5 to 3.8.

dissent An opinion written by a judge expressing disagreement with the decision of the majority in a court case. It is included in the official record of the decision of the court.

emancipation The act of freeing from slavery. In the United States, all slaves were emancipated when the Thirteenth Amendment was ratified in December 1865.

enumerated powers The powers assigned to Congress in Article I of the Constitution.

federal Having to do with the United States government rather than a state or local government.

freedman The term for a former slave.

Great Migration The movement of six million African Americans from the South to other parts of the country between 1916 and 1970.

hearing In the US Senate or House, a meeting or series of meetings, often open to the public, conducted for the purpose of obtaining information.

icon A person who has been in a position for a long time, has been very successful, and is therefore greatly respected.

interstate commerce Economic activity that is conducted between two or more states.

jurisprudence The theory and principles of a legal system.

justice The term for judges on the Supreme Court to set them apart from judges on federal district and circuit courts.

Ku Klux Klan An organization of white extremists that terrorized black people throughout the South in an attempt to maintain white control.

originalism The philosophy of interpreting the meaning of laws and the Constitution on the basis of what the people who wrote the laws (legislators) and the Constitution (Founding Fathers) meant at the time they wrote them.

petitioner In a federal court, a person or other entity that appeals to the court to consider a case.

respondent In a federal court, the party in an appeals case against whom the petitioner made the appeal.

segregate To separate. Segregation was the policy common throughout the southern United States that required separate schools and other facilities for black and white citizens. It was ruled unconstitutional in 1954.

seminary A school for training people to become priests or ministers.

slave codes Laws enacted by colonial governments in America severely restricting many activities of slaves.

solicitor general In the US legal system, the attorney who represents the federal government in cases before the Supreme Court.

stare decisis Latin for "stand by what is decided;" the principle of using past legal decisions as guides for current decisions.

statutory law Laws that have been enacted by a legislature—either Congress or a state legislative body.

textualism A method of interpretation that uses the plain text of the Constitution and laws to understand their meaning.

unorthodox Not in keeping with what is accepted by the majority of people.

uppity Having a superior attitude; behaving as though one is better than he or she really is or should be.

SOURCES

INTRODUCTION

1. 28 US Code § 453.

2. Clarence Thomas, *My Grandfather's Son* (New York: HarperCollins, 2007), 286.

CHAPTER ONE

1. Woodrow Wilson, Address delivered at Joint Session of the Two Houses of Congress, April 2, 1917; US 65th Congress, 1st Session, Senate Document 5.

2. W. E. B Du Bois, "Returning Soldiers," *The Crisis*, XVIII (May, 1919), 13.

3. W. E. B Du Bois, "Returning Soldiers," 13.

CHAPTER TWO

1. Clarence Thomas, *My Grandfather's Son* (New York: HarperCollins, 2007), 28.

2. Clarence Thomas, "Why Black Americans Should Look to Conservative Politics," Speech to the Heritage Foundation, August 1, 1987, http://www.blackpast.org/1987-clarence-thomas-why-black-americans-should-look-conservative-politics.

3. Clarence Thomas, Speech to the National Bar Association, Memphis, TN, July 28, 1998, http://teachingamericanhistory.org/library/document/speech-to-the-national-bar-association, paragraph 34.

4. Juan Williams, "Open Season on Clarence Thomas," *Washington Post*, October 10, 1991, paragraph 1.

5. Hearings Before the Committee on the Judiciary United States Senate One Hundred Second Congress First Session on the Nomination of Clarence Thomas to Be Associate Justice of the Supreme Court of the United States, October 11, 12, and 13, 1991, Part 4, https://www.loc.gov/law/find/nominations/thomas/hearing-pt4.pdf, 157–158.

CHAPTER THREE

1. Cited in Adam Liptic, "From Justice Thomas, a Little Talk about Race, Faith and the Court," *New York Times*, September 17, 2010, https://www.nytimes.com/2012/09/18/us/clarence-thomas-discusses-his-life-and-the-supreme-court.html.

2. Adam Tamburin, "Supreme Court Justice Sonia Sotomayor's Vanderbilt Talk Touched on Clarence Thomas, Bob Dylan," *Tennessean*, April 3, 2018, https://www.tennessean.com/story/news/2018/04/03/sonia-sotomayor-vanderbilt-clarence-thomas/474260002.

3. Emily Newburger, "Justice Thomas Speaks at Harvard Law," *Harvard Law Today*, February 11, 2013, https://today.law.harvard.edu/justice-thomas-speaks-at-harvard-law-video, paragraph 8.

4. Sherman Goldenberg, "Justice Thomas Loves the RV Lifestyle," *RV Business*, June 14, 2004, https://www.rvbusiness.com/2004/06/justice-thomas-loves-the-rv-lifestyle.

CHAPTER FOUR

1. Clarence Thomas, *My Grandfather's Son* (New York: HarperCollins, 2007), 188.

2. Clarence Thomas, "Be Not Afraid," Francis Boyer Lecture, American Enterprise Institute, February 13, 2001, https://www.aei.org/publication/be-not-afraid.

3. *McDonald v. Chicago*, 561 US 742 (2010).

4. *United States v. Lopez*, 514 US 549 (1995).

5. *Gonzalez v. Raich*, 545 US 1 (2005).

6. *Adarand Constructors, Inc. v. Peña*, 515 US 200 (1995).

CHAPTER FIVE

1. Clarence Thomas and John Malcolm, "Joseph Story Distinguished Lecture: A Conversation with Clarence Thomas," November 22, 2017, https://www.heritage.org/courts/report/joseph-story-distinguished-lecture-conversation-clarence-thomas.

2. *Plessy v. Ferguson,* 163 US 537 (1896).

3. Thomas, cited in Adam White, "Clarence Thomas Is Building a Majority by Dissent," *Weekly Standard*, October 26, 2016, https://www.weeklystandard.com/adam-j-white/clarence-thomas-is-building-a-majority-by-dissent.

4. *United States v. Lopez*, 514 US 549 (1995).

5. *McDonald v. Chicago*, 561 US 742 (2010).

6. *McDonald v. Chicago*, 561 US 742 (2010).

7. Clarence Thomas and John Malcolm, "Joseph Story Distinguished Lecture: A Conversation with Clarence Thomas."

8. *Planned Parenthood of Southeastern Pennsylvnia v. Casey*, 505 US 833 (1992).

9. *Gonzales v. Carhart*, 550 US 124 (2007).

10. Clarence Thomas, *My Grandfather's Son* (New York, NY: HarperCollins, 2007), 204.

CHAPTER SIX

1. Adam White, "Clarence Thomas Is Building a Majority by Dissent," *Weekly Standard*, October 26, 2016, https://www.weeklystandard.com/adam-j-white/clarence-thomas-is-building-a-majority-by-dissent.

2. Jeffrey Toobin, "Partners: Will Clarence and Virginia Thomas Succeed in Killing Obama's Health-care Plan?" *New Yorker*, August 29, 2011, https://www.newyorker.com/magazine/2011/08/29/partners-jeffrey-toobin.

3. Ralph Rossum, "Understanding Clarence Thomas: The Jurisprudence of Constitutional Restoration," *Law and Liberty*, April 1, 2014, https://www.lawliberty.org/liberty-forum/understanding-clarence-thomas-the-jurisprudence-of-constitutional-restoration.

FURTHER INFORMATION

BOOKS

Brady, Diane. *Fraternity*. New York: Spiegel and Grau, 2012.

Byers, Ann. *Beyond Slavery: African Americans from Emancipation to Today*. New York: Enslow, 2017.

Foskett, Ken. *Judging Thomas: The Life and Times of Clarence Thomas*. New York: Harper Collins, 2009.

Perritano, John. *Supreme Court*. Costa Mesa, CA: Saddleback Educational Publishing, 2016.

Thomas, Clarence. *My Grandfather's Son*. New York: Harper Collins, 2007.

WEBSITES

Justice Clarence Thomas
http://justicethomas.com

The Justice Clarence Thomas website includes information on his life and his work on the Supreme Court. It includes a biography, links to all of his opinions, and articles and videos giving analysis and detail about his jurisprudence.

Oyez
http://www.oyez.org

A collaborative project of Cornell and Chicago-Kent Law Colleges and Justia, a legal information and research website, Oyez provides authoritative printed and audio records of Supreme Court cases and justices from 1789 to the present.

Supreme Court of the United States
http://www.supremecourt.gov/about/traditions.aspx

The official website of the US Supreme Court presents information about the history and traditions of the court, lists the current justices, and provides details about what the court does and how it operates.

MUSEUMS/ORGANIZATIONS

College of the Holy Cross
1 College Street
Worcester, MA 01610
(508) 793-2011

Pin Point Heritage Museum
9924 Pin Point Ave.
Savannah, GA 31406
(912) 355-0064

Supreme Court Building
1 First St. NE
Washington, DC 20543
(202) 479-3000

Yale University – Mead Visitor Center
149 Elm Street
New Haven, CT 06520
(203) 432-4771

BIBLIOGRAPHY

Adarand Constructors, Inc. v. Peña, 515 US 200 (1995).

Brown, Taylor Kate. "Ruth Bader Ginsburg: Who Are the Nine Supreme Court Justices?" *BBC News Magazine*, June 27, 2018. www.bbc.com/news/magazine-33103973.

Du Bois, W. E. B. "Returning Soldiers," *Crisis*, XVIII (May, 1919).

"Former Clarence Thomas Clerks are a Presence in Trump Administration." CBS News, August 6, 2018. https://www.cbsnews.com/news/former-clarence-thomas-clerks-are-a-presence-in-trump-administration.

Goldenberg, Sherman. "Justice Thomas Loves the RV Lifestyle." *RV Business*, June 14, 2004. http://www.rvbusiness.com/2004/06/justice-thomas-loves-the-rv-lifestyle.

Gonzalez v. Raich, 545 US 1 (2005).

"The Justices of the United States Supreme Court." *Supreme Court Review*. Accessed September 4, 2018. http://supremecourtreview.com/default/justice.

Library of Congress. Supreme Court Nominations: Confirmed. Accessed August 28, 2018. http://www.loc.gov/law/find/court-confirmed.php.

Liptic, Adam "From Justice Thomas, a Little Talk about Race, Faith and the Court." *New York Times*, September 17, 2010. http://www.nytimes.com/2012/09/18/us/clarence-thomas-discusses-his-life-and-the-supreme-court.html.

McDonald v. Chicago, 561 US 742 (2010).

National Association for the Advancement of Colored People. "The History of the NAACP." Accessed August 21, 2018. https://naacp.3cdn.net/14a2d3f78c1910ac31_frm6bev0u.pdf.

Newburger, Emily. "Justice Thomas Speaks at Harvard Law." *Harvard Law Today*, February 11, 2013. https://today.law.harvard.edu/justice-thomas-speaks-at-harvard-law-video.

O'Connor, Sandra Day. "Justice Sandra Day O'Connor on Why Judges Wear Black Robes." *Smithsonian*, November 2013. Accessed August 23, 2018. http://www.smithsonianmag.com/history/justice-sandra-day-oconnor-on-why-judges-wear-black-robes-4370574.

Planalp, Matthew. "The Work of a Supreme Law Clerk." *Cockle Legal Briefs*. Accessed September 4, 2018. http://www.cocklelegalbriefs.com/blog/supreme-court/supreme-court-law-clerks.

Plessy v. Ferguson, 163 U.S. 537 (1896).

Rhode, Deborah L. "Letting the Law Catch Up." *Stanford Law Review* 44, summer 1992, pp. 1259-1265. doi:10.2307/1229058.

Rossum, Ralph. "Understanding Clarence Thomas: The Jurisprudence of Constitutional Restoration." *Law and Liberty*, April 1, 2014. http://www.lawliberty.org/liberty-forum/understanding-clarence-thomas-the-jurisprudence-of-constitutional-restoration.

Ruff, Bob. "Harvard Square Outbreak Overshadows April Demonstrations." *Heights*, April 28, 1970. Accessed August 13, 2018. https://newspapers.bc.edu/?a=d&d=bcheights19700428.2.44.

SCOTUSblog. Statistics. Accessed August 28, 2018. http://www.scotusblog.com/statistics.

Tamburin, Adam, "Supreme Court Justice Sonia Sotomayor's Vanderbilt Talk Touched on Clarence Thomas, Bob Dylan." *Tennessean*, April 3, 2018. http://www.tennessean.com/story/news/2018/04/03/sonia-sotomayor-vanderbilt-clarence-thomas/474260002.

Thomas, Clarence. "Be Not Afraid." Francis Boyer Lecture, American Enterprise Institute, February 13, 2001. http://www.aei.org/publication/be-not-afraid.

———. *My Grandfather's Son*. New York: HarperCollins, 2007.

———. "Why Black Americans Should Look to Conservative Politics." Speech to the Heritage Foundation, August 1, 1987. Accessed August 14, 2018. http://www.blackpast.org/1987-clarence-thomas-why-black-americans-should-look-conservative-politics.

————. "Speech to the National Bar Association, Memphis, TN, July 28, 1998." http://teachingamericanhistory.org/library/document/speech-to-the-national-bar-association/.

Thomas, Clarence, and John Malcolm. "Joseph Story Distinguished Lecture: A Conversation with Clarence Thomas." November 22, 2017. http://www.heritage.org/courts/report/joseph-story-distinguished-lecture-conversation-clarence-thomas.

Toobin, Jeffrey. "The Burden of Clarence Thomas." *New Yorker*, September 27, 1993. https://www.newyorker.com/magazine/1993/09/27/the-burden-of-clarence-thomas.

————. "Partners: Will Clarence and Virginia Thomas Succeed in Killing Obama's Health-care Plan?" *New Yorker*, August 29, 2011. https://www.newyorker.com/magazine/2011/08/29/partners-jeffrey-toobin

Totenberg, Nina. "Sotomayor Found Her 'Competitive Spirit' in Gold Stars." NPR, January 14, 2013. http://www.npr.org/2013/01/14/169363309/sotomayor-found-her-competitive-spirit-in-gold-stars.

United States Courts. "Supreme Court Procedures." Accessed August 21, 2018. http://www.uscourts.gov/about-federal-courts/educational-resources/about-educational-outreach/activity-resources/supreme-1.

United States v. Lopez, 514 US 549 (1995).

White, Adam. "Clarence Thomas Is Building a Majority by Dissent." *Weekly Standard*, October 26, 2016. http://www.weeklystandard.com/adam-j-white/clarence-thomas-is-building-a-majority-by-dissent.

———. "'Just, Wise, and Constitutional': Justice Thomas's Legacy in Law and Politics." *Law and Liberty*, April 17, 2014. www.lawliberty.org/liberty-forum/just-wise-and-constitutional-justice-thomass-legacy-in-law-and-politics.

Williams, Juan. "Open Season on Clarence Thomas," *Washington Post*, October 10, 1991. www.washingtonpost.com/archive/opinions/1991/10/10/open-season-on-clarence-thomas/1126ce5b-c63c-447b-b496-545b198d4dcd/?utm_term=.0e70c279b850.

Wilson, Woodrow. "War Message to Congress, 1917." Address delivered at Joint Session of the Two Houses of Congress, April 2, 1917; US 65th Congress, 1st Session, Senate Document 5. http://wps.prenhall.com/wps/media/objects/107/110495/ch22_a2_d1.pdf.

INDEX

Rehnquist, Chief Justice
    William, **7**, 36, 49–50, 56,
    90, 94–95
respondent, 59, 76, 80–81
riot, 19, 31, **32–33**
Roberts, Chief Justice John,
    49, 50, **92**, 95–96, **95**
Roe v. Wade, 88, **89**, 90
Roosevelt, President Franklin
    D., 22–23

Savannah, 26, 28–30
Scalia, Justice Antonin,
    54–56, **55**, 64, 90, 94, 96
segregate, 6, 14–17, 23,
    28–29, 39, 102
seminary, 28–30
"separate but equal," 15, 23,
    77
sharecropping, 10–12, 16
Shelby County v. Holder, 83

slave codes, 12
slavery, 9-10, 12, 23
solicitor general, 54, 101
Sotomayor, Justice Sonia,
    52–54, **53**, 56
Sowell, Thomas, 39
stare decisis, 86–88
statutory law, 86, 88
swing vote, 48

textualism, 62, 95
Thirteenth Amendment, 12,
    18
Thomas, Virginia Lamp, **4**, **74**

unorthodox, 40
uppity, 19, 44

World War I, 16, **20–21**, 23

ABOUT THE AUTHOR

Ann Byers is an author, editor, and youth worker with a passion for history, especially American history. A graduate of Webster University in St. Louis, Missouri, she has lived on both the east and west coasts, in the Midwest, and in the Southwest. This varied experience has helped her gain an understanding of and appreciation for the richness and diversity of the different cultural strands of American life. Of the books she has written for high school and middle school readers, two that touch on the topics in this book are *Beyond Slavery: African Americans from Emancipation to Today* and *Immigration: Interpreting the Constitution.*